THE ULTIMATE OXBRIDGE COLLEGE GUIDE

UniAdmissions

Copyright © 2020 *UniAdmissions*. All rights reserved.

Previous Editions: 2019, 2018

ISBN 978-1-913683-72-6

No part of this publication may be reproduced or transmitted in any form or by any means, electronic or mechanical, including photocopying, recording, or by any information retrieval system without prior written permission of the publisher. This publication may not be used in conjunction with or to support any commercial undertaking without the prior written permission of the publisher.

Published by RAR Medical Services Limited

www.uniadmissions.co.uk

info@uniadmissions.co.uk

Tel: 0208 068 0438

This book is neither created nor endorsed by the University of Oxford or the University of Cambridge. The authors and publisher are not affiliated with the University of Oxford or the University of Cambridge. The information offered in this book is purely advisory and any advice given should be taken within this context. As such, the publishers and authors accept no liability whatsoever for the outcome of any applicant's interview performance, the outcome of any university applications or for any other loss. Although every precaution has been taken in the preparation of this book, the publisher and author assume no responsibility for errors or omissions of any kind. Neither is any liability assumed for damages resulting from the use of information contained herein. This does not affect your statutory rights.

THE ULTIMATE OXBRIDGE COLLEGE GUIDE

MATTHEW W. ELLIOTT

DR. ROHAN AGARWAL

UniAdmissions

ABOUT THE AUTHOR

Matthew graduated from King's College, London and Emmanuel College, Cambridge. Over the last five years, he has tutored dozens of successful Oxbridge applicants in the UK, Europe, and China.

He has also worked for Oliver Wyman, and Unilever, written for the New Statesman and the Independent, as well as teaching both postgraduates and under-graduates at the Guangxi University for Nationalities in Nanning, China.

Rohan is the **Managing Director** of *UniAdmissions* and is responsible for its technical and commercial arms. He graduated from Gonville and Caius College, Cambridge and is a fully qualified doctor. Over the last five years, he has tutored hundreds of successful Oxbridge and Medical applicants. He has also authored dozens of books on admissions tests and interviews.

Rohan has taught physiology to undergraduates and interviewed medical school applicants for Cambridge. He has published research on bone physiology and writes education articles for the Independent and. In his spare time, Rohan enjoys playing the piano and table tennis.

THE ULTIMATE OXBRIDGE COLLECTION | BASICS

THE BASICS 9
   Course Profiles 14
   Biochemistry at Oxford 15
   Computer Science at Cambridge 19
   Economics and Management at Oxford 25
   Engineering at Cambridge 28
   Engineering At Oxford 32
   Law At Oxford 36
   Medicine at Cambridge 39
   Natural Sciences at Cambridge 42
   Philosophy, Politics, and Economics at Oxford 46
   Psychology at Oxford 51
   Psychology at Cambridge 55
   Veterinary Medicine at Cambridge 58
   Cambridge Colleges 63
      Christ's College 64
      Churchill College 65
      Clare College 66
      Clare Hall 68
      Corpus Christi College 69
      Darwin College 70
      Downing College 70
      Emmanuel College 72
      Fitzwilliam College 73
      Girton College 75
      Gonville and Caius College 77
      Homerton College 79

THE ULTIMATE OXBRIDGE COLLECTION | BASICS

Hughes Hall	81
Jesus College	83
King's College	85
Lucy Cavendish College	87
Magdalene College	88
Murray Edwards College	89
Newnham College	90
Pembroke College	92
Peterhouse	94
Queens' College	96
Robinson College	98
Selwyn College	100
Sidney Sussex College	101
St Catherine's College	104
St Edmund's College	105
St John's College	105
Trinity College	107
Trinity Hall	108
Wolfson College	109
Oxford Colleges	111
Balliol College	112
Brasenose College	113
Christ Church	115
Corpus Christi College	117
Exeter College	118
Green Templeton College	120
Harris Manchester College	122
Hertford College	123

THE ULTIMATE OXBRIDGE COLLECTION — BASICS

Jesus College 125
Keble College 127
Kellogg College 130
Lady Margaret Hall 131
Linacre College 132
Lincoln College 134
Magdalen College 137
Mansfield College 139
Merton College 141
New College 142
Nuffield College 146
Oriel College 147
Reuben College 148
Pembroke College 149
Regent's Park College 151
Somerville College 153
St Anne's College 155
St Antony's College 157
St Catherine's College 157
St Cross College 159
St Edmund Hall 160
St Hilda's College 162
St Hugh's College 163
St John's College 165
St Peter's College 167
The Queen's College 168
Trinity College 170

University College	171
Wadham College	172
Wolfson College	173
Worcester College	175
What is a PPH?	177
Which College Quiz	178
FINAL ADVICE	182

THE BASICS

What are Colleges?

Founded hundreds of years ago, Oxford and Cambridge (and Durham as well), are all organised differently from what we might call a modern university. Instead of being organised around a central authority, Oxford and Cambridge grew into universities over centuries, with new colleges slowly being founded. If you walk into Oxford and ask someone where the university is, they won't be able to tell you, as the whole city is the university!

Each college is governed by its fellows – the academics that work there – and has independence from the university to set its own rules. This makes each college a unique experience. If you study at Oxford or Cambridge, you'll often become a life member of your college (although this varies from college to college) opening up networking opportunities and a lifelong sense of community.

Why do they still exist?

Each college is a miniature university of its own, with its own professors, classes, traditions, and exams. The university is the union of all the colleges – like a football team is the union of all eleven players. While some might think it would be a good idea to reform Oxford and Cambridge along more modern lines, the college system is what gives the universities their character.

It also doesn't hurt that the university only really exists as an agreement between the colleges, so it would be hard for them to use their power to change things. On top of this, there is an old joke that explains how things work at Oxford and Cambridge very nicely.

How many Oxford professors does it take to change a lightbulb?

Change?!

How are the colleges different from one another?

Each college has its own unique history and traditions, which means that differences between them can be quite large. Some colleges go back 800 years and have old fashioned rules that might seem confusing or strange. Others are relatively new, like Wolfson or Kellogg and are based on modern ideas of education that reject some of the Oxbridge traditions. Some colleges have longstanding links with historic public schools and other pride themselves on their history of left-wing politics. Each college is unique, and whichever one you choose, you'll usually find that yours is the best. In this respect colleges are likes football teams – in one sense, they're all the same, but in a more important sense, the one that you support is clearly best!

How should I choose a college?

Choosing a college is the most confusing part of the application process for most students. You probably don't personally know anyone who went to Oxford or Cambridge, let alone someone who has opinions on the merits of all the different colleges. The college websites aren't much help either, as they're all trying to convince you to apply to their college. Most people make a decision based on arbitrary factors – do they have a famous graduate who I admire? Did they do well on University Challenge last year?

There's nothing wrong with choosing Magdalen College, Oxford because your ambition in life is to be the next Oscar Wilde. But college life has probably changed a lot since the 1870s! So, to help you make your decision, we've gathered the best intelligence and insights from current undergraduate students at every Oxford and Cambridge college and put it in this collection. We hope it helps you make a decision, or at least narrow down your options. As we said, everyone ends up loving their own college, so it's nowhere near as fraught a decision as it might seem. And, if you ultimately can't decide, you can make an open application, and leave your college in the lap of the gods.

Can I study any subject at any college?

Some subjects are only taught by a few colleges, as there are only a small number of experts on the subject, and so students applying for that subject should apply to their college. For example, Cambridge is the only place in the UK where you can study Anglo Saxon, Norse and Celtic, and even then, only a few Cambridge colleges, such as Pembroke, offer it. This is only the case for a few subjects, but it's worth checking just to be on the safe side!

Are different colleges better for different subjects?

While some colleges are particularly well known for particular subjects – Trinity College, Cambridge is famous for its mathematicians for example – if a college offers your subject, you can be confident that the teaching there will be top-notch. Certain colleges may have a particularly famous figure teaching at them – say Richard Dawkins or Mary Beard – but the absence of someone who you've seen on TV isn't going to have a negative impact on your experience. Obviously enough, the most famous professors tend to be the busiest, so there's a good chance you wouldn't see much of them anyway.

To compare how different colleges perform in the final exams each year, you can look at the Tompkins Table (for Cambridge) or the Norrington Table (for Oxford). You can find graphs of these over time on Wikipedia, where you'll quickly realise that the variation from year to year is pretty huge. Simply put, all the colleges are good, and full of smart people and academics, so which one did best in the Tompkins Table last year shouldn't be how you make your choice.

How is teaching at Oxbridge different?

Teaching at Oxbridge is done based on a unique system, which dates back centuries. Students on the same course will have lectures and practicals together (at least, if your course has a practical element). These are supplemented by college-based tutorials (at Oxford) or supervisions (at Cambridge). A tutorial/supervision is the same thing at both universities, and are different in name only. They are an individual or small group session with an academic to discuss ideas, ask questions, and receive feedback on your assignments. During these, you will be pushed to think critically about the material from the course in novel and innovative ways. To get the most out of Oxbridge, you need to be able to work in this setting and take criticism with a positive and constructive attitude.

These sessions take place within your college, so with only 120 or so new students in each year group, and a diversity of subjects, you may find yourself in a weekly tutorial with an expert with only two or three other students.

What is it like to study at Oxford or Cambridge?

To make this collection a useful as possible, we've tried to put the experiences of real students at the centre of it, rather than factual information you could just find on Wikipedia or the Oxford and Cambridge websites. There are lots of resources encouraging you to apply to Oxford or Cambridge, and there's no shortage of excellent books that you can read to help you write your personal statement, prepare for admissions tests, practice for your interview, and every other aspect of your application. We've even provided a reading list at the back of this collection with a few of our favourites.

Instead, we've gathered information from dozens of current students and recent graduates to find out what they thought of the experience. We've put together eight testimonials for some of the most popular Oxbridge courses, to give you a sense of what it's actually like to study them. We've then prepared profiles of each undergraduate college at Oxford and Cambridge, with help from current students, to give you a taste of what it's actually like to be a member.

THE ULTIMATE OXBRIDGE COLLECTION | BASICS

Of course, everyone experiences the world in their own unique way, and no two people's experiences are the same. However, we hope that in grouping together a range of stories and assessments, you'll be able to get a sense of whether Oxford or Cambridge is right for you, and which college you might make your first choice when you come to apply.

This collection doesn't try to tell you everything you need to know to get into Oxford or Cambridge, how to decide between PPE and Medicine, or a thousand other questions about the process of applying to university. All we're trying to do is answer the most frequently asked questions about Oxbridge: what are the colleges, and how do I pick one?

COURSE PROFILES

What is it like to study at Oxford or Cambridge?

Along with choosing a college, the other big question you'll be facing is what degree do you want to do. Every degree at every university is unique, and Oxbridge is no different in that respect. Some of these differences are quite subtle, so it's important to do your research properly. The university websites will always be the most up to date resource for this, so we haven't tried to reproduce their depth of breadth of information here.

What we've done instead is tried to give you a taste of what studying some of the most popular — and competitive — courses at Oxbridge is like on a daily, weekly, or monthly basis. So, over the next few pages you'll find profiles of some of the most popular courses, written by current students and recent grads, to give you a flavour of what it's actually like.

If you'd like to know more, please do get in touch through the *UniAdmissions* website, where we'll be able to help you with every aspect of your application, including informal conversations with current students to help you decide which course is the right fit for you.

Degree Profiles

BIOCHEMISTRY AT OXFORD

This testimonial is by Aditi Shringarpure, a tutor with UniAdmissions, and a third-year in Biochemistry at Exeter College, Oxford.

The course is 4 years long; comprising of 3 years of undergraduate teaching and the 4th year as an integrated masters during which you complete an independent lab project. In first year, you study 5 compulsory courses: Cellular, Molecular, Mechanistic, Physical and Quantitative Biochemistry. In second and third year, the teaching is based around 5 compulsory themes (Toolboxes for biochemistry, Information transfer in biological systems, Molecular processes in the cell, Cellular chemistry and The cell in time and space) which build on the knowledge from first year. In second and third year you are more in touch with the current state of the research in these areas and which aspects are being explored. In addition to learning new concepts in second and third year, you also gain a greater understanding of the experimental techniques which are deployed to gain these insights. This is good preparation for the fourth year which is predominantly practical, and lab based. Your fourth year research project is integrated with the work of a lab in Oxford, and you become part of the lab group for 23 weeks full time. There are a variety of projects to choose from covering research areas that have been taught during the second and third year offered by the Biochemistry department but also many to choose from in labs at the Dunn School of Pathology, Wellcome Centre for Human Genetics, Kennedy Institute of Rheumatology as well as other clinically focused projects at the Oxford University Trust Hospitals. In addition to the lab research project, you also write a review article on a different area of research of your choice as coursework.

The course is assessed by formal written exams at the end of the first and third year in June, with 4 2-hour summative assessments during the course of the second and third year as well. Assessment in fourth year is based on the dissertation and presentation of the research project and coursework review article. The exams at the end of first year are called Prelims and consist of 5 written papers; 1 on each of the courses mentioned above. To proceed to second year, Prelims need to be passed but the results from these exams do not count towards your overall degree. However, if you achieve over 70%, you are awarded a distinction and depending on the college, scholarship prizes in the form of credits towards college expenses or book vouchers. Prelims papers are a mixture of essay papers and extended response questions (Cellular and Molecular Biochemistry) as well as short-answer biophysical and calculation-based papers (Physical and Quantitative Biochemistry). Completion of first and third year also requires a satisfactory practical record. The exams at the end of third year are called Finals and consist of 7 written papers; 1 essay paper on each of the courses mentioned above as well as a general essay paper. The seventh paper is a Data Analysis and Interpretation paper which involves interpreting experimental results, drawing graphs and some calculations.

What is it like to study?

The course workload is quite heavy, particularly in first year which has the greatest number of contact hours as well as the highest number of deadlines per week. In first year you typically have 12-13 hours of lectures per week which reduces to 6-7 hours in second and third year. In addition to lectures in first year, you also attend classes, tutorials and practicals. The following is an outline of a typical day in first year.

Lectures 9-12

Lectures are typically 50 minutes long with a 5-minute break between each in the block of 3.

Until COVID-19, lectures were not recorded so could only be listened to in person. During the pandemic, lectures have been pre-recorded and uploaded online though whether this persists after COVID is unclear. Lecture handouts are provided usually with copies of the slides used by the lecturer but others can be the lecturer's hand-drawn diagrams which you can annotate.

Classes: 2-3 pm

Classes for a course take place with another college and you usually go through a worksheet that you have handed in advance. The worksheets are helpful practice for applying concepts taught in lectures and getting used to some exam-style questions.

Tutorials: 5-7 pm

Tutorials are small group teaching sessions (one or two other students) usually with a college Biochemistry tutor once or twice a week. You prepare an essay about a topic in the course in detail to discuss. Tutorials are an opportunity to both consolidate the lecture material and strengthen your understanding of a topic as well as go beyond the lecture reading list. The primary sources for essays in first year are lecture handouts and textbooks whilst in second- and third-year journal articles are the main focus along with some specialist textbooks specific to lecture series.

Post 7 pm:

After contact hours for the day, you often have to work on the tutorial essays, worksheets or practical write up due for the week. Heading to the library can be helpful and a more motivating setting to work in after a day of contact hours. Alternatively, the comfort of working in your room has its benefits like easily making a cup of tea.

Labs: 10 am-4 pm

Once a week in first year you have practical labs for about 5-6 hours during which you complete a few different experiments which use a similar technique or investigate a topic covered in the lectures. You work through your lab book experiments and answer questions with your lab partner and complete a write up due the following week. During the experiments, you can ask the demonstrators any questions, ask for help with practical set-up and talk through your results with them. In second and third year, you have fewer labs (2-3 per term) but they last two days. Whilst in first year labs, you follow a set-out protocol, second- and third-year labs involve more experimental design where you plan the experiment to show or test the concepts specified in the lab book.

Application process

In addition to the UCAS application, if selected you come to Oxford for at least two interviews: one at the college you applied to and one at a randomly allocated college. The structure of the interview depends on the college and the tutor conducting them. Whilst the problems may seem very complex at first, take them one step at a time and as you are thinking, explain your logic and the assumptions you are making. The tutors are more interested in understanding how you think and the approaches you use to problem solve rather than getting the correct answer. Some may discuss part of your personal statement and so being prepared to discuss it would be a good idea. Other interviews can include discussing an article or data that you are given half an hour before.

COMPUTER SCIENCE AT CAMBRIDGE

This article was contributed by Anoushka Mazumdar, a tutor with UniAdmissions, and a second-year in Computer Science at Churchill College.

Course Structure

The Bachelor's course is a three year course (the three years are called Part IA, IB and II), but there is an optional integrated Master's with a fourth year (Part III). To gain admissions on the Master's program you have to achieve a first class at your third year final exams.

The full range of courses and options is available online, but some of the main differences between the three years is described below.

First Year (Part IA)

There are four papers taken at the end of this year, one of which is the Maths Paper. The lectures for this Maths paper are taken alongside the Natural Sciences Tripos, and there is an option to take Maths A or Maths B. Maths B is aimed at those who studied Further Maths at A level, with the lectures moving at a slightly faster pace, and more content being covered. This will give you a greater choice of questions to answer in the final exam, but both Maths A and Maths B students take the same final paper. The other three papers are from the Computer Science Tripos and are all assessed in the form of written exam at the end of the year. There are no course choices this year.

Second Year (Part IB)

There are four papers in the final exam, all for Computer Science at the end of the year. All students must attend all lectures, however, there is a choice between topics to answer questions in the exam. There is also a group project that runs in the second term (Lent term) where students are in a group of 6-7, and work with a client for two months to deliver a product or service according to their specifications. This is aimed to give students more practical experience and learn teamwork.

Third Year (Part II)

Whilst this year also has results based on final examination, you are also required to complete an independent Part II project on a topic of your choice. In this you will have a supervisor to give you advice through the project, and will also produce a dissertation by the end. The mark from your part II project will count towards your final class for third year. There is also choice on two optional modules to take, which will be examined after you complete them during the year instead of in the final exam.

Assessment and Practical Work

The classes (1st, 2.i, 2.ii, 3rd, fail) are given based on end of year examinations (slightly different for 3rd year, detailed above). There is also practical coursework (called ticks) to be completed throughout the degree for the courses that require them. If you do not pass a practical then there will be marks deducted from your final exam score, however, everyone typically passes all of their practical work.

What is it like to Study there?

Lectures

The first year was particularly challenging, since I came with barely any background knowledge in Computer Science. However, at the end of the first year everyone is brought up to the same level. Currently as a second year, I have found that understanding of the course content comes much more quickly. Almost all lectures happen in the morning (most after 10 am) with a few running into the afternoon. In the first year we had 11 lectures a week (including Maths). This second year we have had 13 per week but fewer towards the end of the 2nd term to allow for time to work on the group project. Most first year lectures are located away from the Computer Lab, but from second year onwards almost all lectures will be in the Lab in West Cambridge. (Might be a factor to consider for college choice, depending on how much you like cycling).

Practical Work

In my opinion this is one of the best parts of the degree since you are able to implement your knowledge from lectures and some of my fondest memories are working on practical tasks together with my friends in the lab. There is some group or pair work such as the group project (Part IB) and hardware labs (Part IA), however, most of it is individual. For the majority of the practicals you are able to work at your own time and location, and upload your code for an online automated tester within a limited time frame. However, I still found it incredibly useful and fun to work with my friends to discuss problems and solutions together. The frequency of practicals depends on the courses in the timetable for that term and is very variable for each term.

Supervisions

The number of supervisions for each course greatly depends on the college. I had 4 supervisions a week in the first year, however, in the second year the frequency has been less. It is very common to have weekend supervisions, however, they require you to submit the work beforehand which actually avoids you working in the weekend. A typical supervision is a one hour long class with two people and the supervisor. The supervisor will give you a set of questions to complete and submit beforehand. These will be marked and explained in the supervision. The supervision is also your chance to ask about any other parts of the course you don't understand, or anything further you want to discuss outside the scope of the lectures.

For us, we have the freedom to schedule our own supervisions. This can allow flexibility if you are behind with a certain course, but you also have to be careful to manage your time well and structure your term. Other colleges may not have this system of booking supervisions, and a time for the class would be scheduled by the supervisor. If you are in a large college then you can expect your supervision partners to be from the same college, however, for smaller colleges your partner may be from a different college.

Evening Time / Relaxation

It is really important to keep some time for socialising or relaxing in the week. You can join a club, attend formal dinners, and college events, be with friends, hang out in the games room etc. Whilst the workload may vary during the term, meaning there will be some nights spent in the library, there is time for fun as well. I find that having breaks like this often leads to more productive work overall.

Application Process

Personal Statement

In the personal statement they want to see passion for the subject. Since Computer Science A-Level is not compulsory, the interviewers would like you to demonstrate something you have done on your own to realise that Computer Science is a subject that you would like to study. This could include personal projects, or learning to code via problem solving e.g. Project Euler questions, work experiences, clubs inside or outside of school, hackathons or other coding competitions, courses (in person or online), contributing to open source projects, giving a technical presentation, participating in a computer related summer camp, reading relevant books etc. These are a few examples I could think of, but anything that involved you learning independently about Computer science enough to spark an interest would qualify. There is not a certain level of technical knowledge that you need since the university knows everyone comes from different backgrounds. The colleges are also looking for a strong mathematical foundation so also be sure to include anything that demonstrates good problem solving skills or shows your aptitude in Mathematics.

Admissions Assessment

All colleges will require you sit the CTMUA (also known as TMUA) admissions assessment, before you are called for an interview. This is in the format of two multiple choice papers, the first one having a focus on pure maths, and the second one containing more generic problem solving and logic type questions. There are a number of (C)TMUA papers available online for practice, however, if you complete all of these the Oxford MAT paper would be good practice for extra material. Some colleges (named on Cambridge or individual college websites) additionally require you to sit the CSAT paper at interview. This has a much different style of questions with much lengthier questions and requires written solutions. The focus here is on problem solving approaches and whether you can work through a complex problem. If you run out of CSAT practice material, then STEP questions are a good source of similar problems.

Interview

There are typically one or two half an hour interviews depending on the college. In these you will be asked one or two maths or problem solving type questions with the problem becoming harder and harder the more you progress through them. For this reason don't expect to know everything at interview or to be able to answer everything, because they will keep increasing the difficulty of the question in the time given. Throughout the interview it is important that you constantly think aloud and narrate why you are taking each step. This will help them understand how you are approaching the problem and help them guide you back on track if you go wrong. The problems can be deliberately vague so be sure to ask clarifying questions, and always attempt to offer up a solution or approach even though it might not be the best one. The interviewer will help you improve on it.

If you have multiple interviews then they might ask you about your personal statement, but this is again a chance for you to show your interest in the subject. There is no level of expected knowledge in Computer Science before you apply.

ECONOMICS AND MANAGEMENT AT OXFORD

This testimonial is by Gideon Blankstone, a 1st year student in Economics & Management at Pembroke College, Oxford.

How is the course structured?

Economics and Management (E&M) is a three year degree and students will receive a BA upon completion. There are three modules in first year, all of which are compulsory. These are Introductory Economics, Financial Management, and General Management. Introductory Economics is taught over the first 2 terms, with one of microeconomics and macroeconomics studied in each. Financial management is also taught over 2 terms, being split between financial reporting (accounting) and financial analysis (more similar to corporate finance). General management is also taught over 2 terms, but it is cumulative throughout the module. First year ends with Preliminary Examinations (prelims) which must be passed to advance to Final Honours School (FHS). There will be college organised exams known as collections at the start of every term, apart from the first term as a fresher, to allow for exam practice and for the college to ensure that students are remaining on top of their work. The marks in these papers have no bearing on the prelims results or final degree classification. The entire prelims grade is based on a formal written assessment at the end of the summer term.

Once prelims have been passed, students advance to FHS and are given a wide range of modules from which to pick. Second- and third-year students can decide from a multitude of options for both economics and management, with a minimum of 2 modules and a maximum of six from one discipline. There is the option for a dissertation written in third year. The grade achieved in prelims or any collections has no bearing on the final degree classification, so even if a student struggles in first year, there is no panic for getting a low classification as there is a large range of choice for students to tailor their degrees best suited to their skills. Most modules are assessed as written exams, with a select few as projects or extended essays.

THE ULTIMATE OXBRIDGE COLLEGE GUIDE | DEGREE PROFILES

What is it like to study?

During first year, a typical week would include between 4-6 lectures, two tutorials and a class.

Introductory economics is taught through lectures and tutorials. Lectures are held at the Examination Schools on High Street, and are run alongside the PPE course as well as History and Economics (HECO). There would typically be 2-4 economics lectures per week, lasting for an hour. Students will also have roughly one tutorial per week (though the regularity is determined by specific college tutor). Tutorials are held with one professor and between 2-4 students from the same college. Tutors will set work to be handed in and will often use tutorials to ensure students are understanding all the content. Economics tutors mostly set problem sheets and essays, and these are often discussed in tutorials, along with any other relevant content. For students who feel they may need greater help with the mathematics involved in the module, there is a small, non-compulsory and non-assessed maths course that can be taken by anyone who wants.

General Management is taught through 1 two hour lecture at the Said Business school, as well as a tutorial per week. These tutorials have the same format as Introductory Economics, with the work set being an essay per week, alongside a recommended reading list.

Financial management is also taught with 1 two hour lecture per week and a class with roughly 15 students instead of a tutorial. The tutors for these classes will also set work every week, and classes will be used to ensure students were able to understand the problem sheet.

Despite sounding difficult, the workload for E&M is manageable if your time is managed well, with very few contact hours allowing for plenty of time for students to complete their work. Students can use the central university library as well as the Social sciences library or the Business School library. Each college also has a library so there are plenty of places to work or find resources for essays or problem sheets.

A major advantage of being an E&M student is the access to the Saïd Business School. The business school is next to the train station and is within a 20 minute walk from any college. It has a very large and well-resourced library that has plenty of space for individual quiet work as well as a space for group working. There are also 2 cafés in the business school which allow unlimited free tea and coffee for students, as well as newspapers such as the Financial Times.

Overall, the course is challenging but very rewarding, and the workload allows for time to pursue other interests beyond the scope of the degree.

What is the application process like?

The typical entry requirements for E&M is A*AA, with a minimum of an A in A-Level mathematics, or equivalent in other qualifications. Students apply through UCAS as an early applicant, with either an application to a specific college or an open application. Students are expected to have a strong personal statement showing their strengths and interest in the subject. Oxford University places little emphasis on non-academic achievements.

Once the UCAS application has been completed, students must take the TSA parts 1&2. Part 1 consists of 50 multiple choice questions, split evenly between problem solving and critical thinking – candidates have 90 minutes for this section. Part 2 is a choice of four essay questions, with candidates answering 1 with a 30 minute time allowance and 2 sides of A4 only.

If a high enough score is achieved on the TSA, and the candidate has a strong UCAS application, they will be invited to interview at a college. Students will stay for at least 2 nights in an Oxford college and will have at least 2 interviews, as well as take part in social activities and eat in the dining hall with other applicants. Some students will interview at a second or third college. The interviews are designed to replicate a tutorial, with a focus on a dialogue between student and tutor. They are meant to be difficult, and students aren't expected to get every answer correct. They are used so tutors can understand the suitability of a candidate to the course and adapt to the teaching style at Oxford.

ENGINEERING AT CAMBRIDGE

This testimonia is by Rushabh Shah, a 2nd year student in Engineering at Emmanuel College, Cambridge.

How is the course structured?

The University of Cambridge engineering course is 4 years and is an integrated masters, meaning you graduate with both a Bachelors and Masters degree (BA and Meng). The first two years of the course are general and there is a very limited choice in modules whereas the last two years are where you specialise and choose all the modules you do.

Throughout your time at Cambridge you will be assessed through projects, labs, coursework and summer exams. The marks from these will form your grade each year. Exams taken at the end of the year will, however, contribute a bigger part of the overall grade. Labs and projects will take place during term time and projects often last 4 weeks. Coursework can take place in term time and during breaks.

In the first year the course is broken into 4 parts and these are the 4 papers you will sit: Mechanical Engineering, Structures and Materials, Electrical & Information Engineering and Mathematical Methods. The Mathematical Methods paper includes computing for your first year. Computing is taught through various projects. These start off as teach yourself exercises and progress to induvial and group projects, there is typically 3 computing projects a year for your first two years, including a summer project.

Your second year at Cambridge will build on what you learnt during your first year and is now split into eighths. These are Mechanical Engineering, Structural Engineering, Materials, Thermofluid Mechanics, Electrical Engineering, Information Engineering, Mathematical Methods and finally Business and Electives. The Electives is where you are given your first chance to choose 2 modules relating to the engineering disciplines you have learnt about. Computing in second year is not formally assessed like in first year but rather solely assessed through computing projects linking to topics you are taught.

In your third and fourth year you will choose 10 and 8 modules from a choice of 80+, so you are able to really specialise into something very specific or keep your choices broad. You have to do a certain number of modules of a given discipline (e.g. Mechanical Engineering) to have a degree in that discipline, but the vast number of modules means there are lots of modules relating to various disciplines. It is your choice how specialised you are.

The department is only a short walk and an even shorter cycle ride away from most colleges and this is where you will spend most of your time regarding engineering.

What is it like to study?

A typical day will include various things such as lectures, labs and supervisions and here is what that could look like:

Usually you are given lecture notes with gaps to fill in. These might be the answer to an example, key words or definitions. Lectures are the main source of new information, all the content that you need for the exams in summer will be covered here. A good thing is quite a few are recorded and available online, which is extremely useful for revision and understanding the lecture better. Filled in notes are also made available online.

Labs are related to the topics you cover in lecture and are a good way to see many of the theories you learn about applied in real life and the practical use of equations etc. Everything in the labs is taught from scratch so do not worry if you have limited or no experience with equipment or methods. There are 2 types of labs- long and short. A long lab requires a lab report or some form of written work to be handed in after the lab whereas as short labs finish in the 2-hour slot. Sometimes lab slots are filled by projects such as the structural design project (SDP) and the integrated design project (IEP). These projects will take up all your labs slots for the duration of the project (anywhere between 1-4 weeks). One of the good things about labs in your first and second year is standard credit. This means as long as the work is done to a satisfactory standard you will receive the standard amount of marks available to pass. This does not apply to 3rd and 4th year.

You will have 2 – 3 supervisions a week. They are the only form of teaching organised by your college. A supervision consists of 1-3 students and a fellow (ranging from a PhD student to a world leading professor). During a supervision you will go over an example paper (you will usually get 2-3 of these a week). These are problem sheets which will cover material seen in lectures. Doing example papers will be the bulk of the work you are required to do during term and the bulk of your independent study. Supervisions give you a chance to consolidate your understanding and ask about any questions you had difficulty with. Supervisions are one of the things that makes Cambridge so great.

You will often find you have to do some work in the evenings but don't worry you will have plenty of time to relax and do sociable things such as going to the college bar, going out with friends, going to formal dinners, going to society meets etc.

A typical day is likely to have 3-5 contact hours. This is an average day and so some days will be less full. You will not have labs every day of the week (only 2 or 3 times) for example. Similarly, you will only have supervisions 2 -3 times a week. The engineering department has a library with various books related to the course and beyond, for extra reading or if you want to work a bit harder on a specific area. Your college will also have a library with engineering material, but this will be in a lower volume. All the lecture content and examples papers will be available online as well as in handouts and between this, supervisions and use of the library you will not have to go looking far to answer any questions you have.

The breadth of the course means you learn about lots of different aspects of engineering and this can often change your outlook and opinions about what you want to do. Often undergraduates arrive in the first year sure of what they want to do, and this is changed by the time they choose modules in third year. The breadth of the course also means that if you have no idea what to specialise in then you are given the chance to explore different avenues before choosing.

There are also lots of extracurricular clubs and societies run by students and these build and explore things such as rockets, racing cars and many more. You will also be allowed to use the Dyson Centre which houses various machines and materials allowing you to undertake any extra projects you want to. There are lots of other non-subject related societies available in Cambridge so you will never find yourself bored and looking for things to do.

What is the application process like?

When you apply to Cambridge you apply to one of the 31 colleges available (or alternatively you can do an open application and be assigned a college). Overall, the colleges have basically the same entry requirements of A*A*A* and the subjects they usually look for are maths and physics, some colleges also want further maths and this is a definite advantage. You will also have to sit an admissions test in November called the ENGAA. This tests your knowledge of maths and physics and is a multiple choice test. After this test the college will get back to you and either offer you an interview or unfortunately reject you. Interviews vary from college to college largely and some require you to sit a test on the day of the interview as well. The interview will further test your knowledge in maths, physics and engineering. After this you will either be offered a place subject to meeting the entry requirements or you will be unfortunately rejected. Each college is different and so it is worth looking at the college's website for more specific information.

ENGINEERING AT OXFORD

This testimonial is by Akshay Pal, a 2nd year student in Engineering at St Hilda's College, Oxford.

How in the course structured?

The Engineering Science course is a 4 year integrated masters course meaning you will graduate with an MEng (Masters in Engineering) degree. The first and second years cover a broad range of topics across many engineering disciplines. In these years you will study four papers which are Mathematics, Electrical and Information Engineering, Structures Mechanics and Dynamics and Energy Systems. All four papers are compulsory in both first and second year and there are no optional modules. In the third year you begin to specialise and will take a number of optional papers, along with one compulsory paper called "Engineering in Society" and two projects. There are around fifteen optional papers which cover a wide range of engineering disciplines including mechanical, civil, biomedical, chemical and information engineering. From the choice of fifteen you will choose five papers to sit. The two projects are an "Engineering Computation" project where you use numerical methods in MATLAB (a programming environment) to solve a given engineering problem. You will have lectures before the project which teach you everything you need to know about MATLAB and programming so don't worry if you've never written code before! The second project in third year is a larger group project known as your 3YP. This is a big project where you design a solution to an engineering problem in a group and work on not just engineering but also topics such as finance, presentation skills, project management and engineering ethics. Another route you can take in third year is the EEM (Engineering, Economics and Management) pathway. This is very similar to the normal third year pathway, you still have two projects and the compulsory "Engineering in Society" paper, however, instead of choosing five topics you only choose four. In place of that fifth topic you will instead take courses in project management, innovation, entrepreneurship and strategy.

In the fourth and final year you have one individual research project (4YP) which accounts for half of your fourth year grade. You also take six optional papers from a selection of about twenty which again cover a whole host of engineering fields.

The course is largely assessed through formal written examinations, however, every year you will also complete lab coursework. The first and second years have no project work so assessment in these years is based solely on your examinations and lab coursework in each year. You will have examinations every year. Similar to most other universities your first year grade does not count towards your final degree classification, however, you must pass the year in order to progress to second year.

What is it like to study?

The workload at Oxford, and Engineering specifically, should not be underestimated, however, it is definitely manageable. Our lectures tend to take place in the mornings, either a 9am or 11am start (with between 8 and 12 lectures weekly in the first year), alongside roughly two tutorials a week in the afternoon. For each lecture course you will complete one problem sheet and normally this will be handed in to your tutors the day before your tutorial. Tutorials in engineering are usually two- or three-on-one sessions with professors in that field of study. Typically they will last an hour and your problem sheet will be the focus of the tutorial as you go through any mistakes you made/difficulties you had. Engineering tutorials are very student led as you need to identify the areas to work on during the tutorial and ask for the help you may need! Tutorials are where you learn as lectures are recapped and difficulties are clarified! Engineers will also have labs around once a week which is normally an all-day affair typically being 11-5 with a one hour break for lunch! On days where your afternoon is empty you can get on with independent study or on Wednesdays get involved with university sport.

This all may sound very daunting and intense, however, there is still plenty of time to get involved in social activities such as playing sport, joining a music ensemble, or any of the various societies at the University. I personally am a member of St. Hilda's Boat Club, St. Hilda's Badminton Club and University College Chapel Choir. The key to balancing everything is good organisation and effective time management which you will quickly pick up as an Oxford student.

The Oxford Experience

Oxford is an extremely easy place to work as the university is home to over 100 libraries making it the largest library system in the UK! This includes central libraries such as the Bodleian and the Radcliffe Camera (affectionately named RadCam), department libraries which for engineers is the Radcliffe Science library and your own college library! This means there is always a new fresh place to work if you get fed up or frustrated of working in the same environment easily and a nice way to explore other colleges is to work in their college library, provided that you have a friend there that can let you in!

Along with the academic facilities, Oxford has bustling streets with plenty of bars, restaurants, and cafes to relax in and even work in, this includes the Westgate shopping centre which has many high-street clothing retailers along with a cinema and minigolf! It also has an excellent night-life with a number of different student nights each week.

The greatest strength of the Oxford Engineering course, in my opinion, is the broad aspect of the first two years, which has given me a wide knowledge and an excellent foundational basis in the core engineering disciplines. When I was applying to universities I was unsure what type of engineering I wished to study and hence the general nature of the course at Oxford was a perfect fit for me as it gave me two years to lay a good foundation upon which I could make an informed decision. I am going into third year in October 2020 and I have chosen options in biomedical and information engineering that, as a sixth form student, I didn't know even existed!

What was the application process like?

The typical entry requirements are A*A*A at A level, or the equivalent in other qualifications. All colleges require A level Mathematics and A level Physics, competitive applicants will often have Further Mathematics as a fourth subject (this is not compulsory but highly recommended). This is due to the highly mathematical nature of engineering. Applicants are required to take a pre-interview written assessment (called the 'PAT') which is a paper on mathematics and physics, and if successful are invited to interview. Interviews are supposed to simulate a tutorial, giving the interviewers a better idea of your suitability to the course and learning style at Oxford. If invited to interview you will have at least two interviews at two different colleges. One of them will be a longer interview focusing on your personal statement and going through a couple of maths and physics problems. The second interview will be shorter and will be focussed on solving one or two longer answer engineering problems. Although the application process is rigorous and extremely demanding, I found that it really enabled me to better understand what I enjoy most about the subject, and why I really wanted to study Engineering.

LAW AT OXFORD

This testimonial is by William Urulako, who graduated with a BA in Law from Christ Church, Oxford in 2019. He is currently training for the Bar exam.

How is the course structured?

Oxford University offers two different Law courses: the standard three-year degree and the four-year Law with Law Studies in Europe degree, which includes a year abroad. You may have noticed that Oxford's Law course is referred to as "Jurisprudence". Do not let this name confuse you; the course is still a qualifying law degree and you will cover much of the same content as you would at other universities. In this context, it refers to the study of law, but it can also refer to legal philosophy.

The course is split into two main parts: Mods and Finals. "Mods" is the name given to the courses you will study in your first two terms at Oxford. You will study Criminal, Constitutional, and Roman Law, and have exams in these subjects just before your Easter vacation. These exams do not count towards your final degree classification, but you need to pass them before progressing to the next stage of your degree.

At the beginning and end of your first year, you will participate in Oxford's Legal Research Skills and Mooting Programme. This is a very minor part of the course and you will learn how to use legal databases and libraries for your research in your first few weeks as an undergraduate. At the end of your first year, you will participate in a moot, which is a bit like a mock trial, only you are arguing a point of law, rather than arguing about the evidence.

Once you are back from your vacation, you will start studying compulsory Finals papers. You must study courses in Tort, Contract, Trusts, Land, Administrative, and European Union Law, as well as a course on Jurisprudence (i.e. legal philosophy). You will take exams in all these papers at the end of your final year. As well as these exams, you will also have to complete a 4,000-word extended essay on Jurisprudence during the summer of your second year, and will be able to choose which topic you write about.

In addition to these courses, you will have two optional modules that are taken during your final year. There is a lot of scope to study different areas of law, such as Company Law, Public International Law, or Media Law, or to take a slightly different module, such as Moral and Political Philosophy. Some of these courses are assessed by an extended essay and others are assessed by a written exam taken at the end of your third year.

If you are studying for the Law with Law Studies in Europe course, you will spend your third year in either the Netherlands, France, Germany, Italy, or Spain, studying the law of that country, or, in the case of the Netherlands, focussing on European Law.

What is it like to study?

Law has a reputation for having a high workload, and this reputation is well-deserved. The usual amount of work you would be expected to do is in the region of 45 hours per week, though some tutors will expect substantially more than that. It is, of course, possible to get by on much less than 45 hours, but this might result in frantic cramming come exam time, which is not recommended!

The course is taught primarily through tutorials, in which one tutor teaches about two students. You will discuss topics that came up in the reading for that week's tutorial and may discuss the essay you submitted in advance of the tutorial. Some courses, particularly modules taken as options in your final year, may be taught with a mixture of tutorials and seminars, which will normally have around ten students and one or more tutors leading a class discussion. Tutorials and seminars usually take up around two hours per week.

As well as tutorials, there will be around 12 hours of lectures per week. Though you should go to these, many students treat them as optional and only go if they feel that they benefit from going. The opportunity to be lectured by world-class academics, Supreme Court judges, and other major figures in the legal world is a fantastic opportunity, so attendance is strongly encouraged!

Owing to the relatively low amount of contact time, there is a lot of flexibility in terms of how you organise your days. Some students might start the day with a rowing session, whereas others might sleep in after a big night out the previous evening. There is not really a typical day for a Law student, but most days will involve at least a few hours of work. There is definitely time to fit in sports, societies, and general leisure time, but you need to be relatively well organised to fit this in around your tutorial work.

Your weekly work will consist of reading and preparing an essay in advance of a tutorial, with tutorials taking place once or twice a week. The University provides you with access to the major legal databases and you will have access to textbooks and other materials centrally at the Law Faculty. Your college is likely to have either a relevant section in its library or may even have a dedicated law library.

What is the application process like?

Typically, you need to take the Law National Admissions Test ('LNAT') and get in the high twenties in its multiple-choice section, produce a strong LNAT essay, have good GCSEs, and submit an excellent personal statement to get to interview. If you get called to interview, you are likely to be asked a range of problem-based questions, usually by two or more academics per interview and usually over the course of two interviews. If you perform well at interview, the typical A-level offer is AAA, with no particular subjects being required.

Studying Law at Oxford is a challenge, but it is a varied course with plenty of different areas to keep you interested. Your capacity for hard work is likely to increase, and your analytical skills are likely to be honed. You will approach problems in a more critical way and your debating skills will improve. Despite being one of the most competitive courses to gain admission to, I would strongly encourage anyone to apply that thinks that it might be the course for them.

MEDICINE AT CAMBRIDGE

This testimonial is by Shirali Patel, a 2nd year medical student at Churchill College, Oxford.

How is the course structured?

The six year course is split in half, into pre-clinical and clinical years. In the pre-clinical section of the course, the first two years are spent studying modules that contribute to your medical degree and the third year is an intercalated year where you pick which subject you would like to study (which does not affect your medical degree). In the first and second year, all modules are compulsory and there is not much scope for choosing what to revise as the multiple-choice can have questions taken from any part of the year. This is not unusual for a subject like Medicine, however, the depth of Science learned at Cambridge can be considerably more rigorous than other institutions. A comprehensive and up-to-date list of modules can be found on the University website but the sometimes-cryptic names essentially mean core topics consist of: anatomy, biochemistry, physiology (first year) and pharmacology, neurobiology, human reproduction, and head & neck anatomy (second year). Additionally, some clinical strands of modules are: epidemiology, ethics (first year) and coursework based on meetings with patients (various points throughout the three years). It can initially seem quite confusing, but the fact that they are all compulsory means it's very easy to find help from your peers as everyone is studying exactly the same thing!

The assessment for the first two years is largely by formal written exams and these are a mix of multiple-choice questions (which allow you to pass on to clinical school) and essays (which contribute to what class you get given at the end of the year). Most Universities do not award classes to medical students, and whilst it is encouraged to aim as high as possible, many people find it comforting that only multiple-choice questions define whether you pass or fail the second component, as essay writing is not everyone's strong suit. Most exams are at the end of the year, which gives you ample time to catch up if you fall behind during term, but some of the "easier" modules (head & neck anatomy, epidemiology and ethics) are assessed at the end of the second term.

The main difference to the course structure is the very limited patient contact you get in the first three years. You should have a think about whether this is how you want to approach studying Medicine as for some, it can be a bit disheartening having solid theoretical learning for three years. However, many find that an upside to this is that by the time you enter clinical environments, you are more confident in your knowledge and learning. Additionally, there are plenty of societies and opportunities to get clinical exposure during these years if you want to, and your Director of Studies and college supervisors can be good contacts to this end.

What is it like to study?

The workload at Cambridge should never be underestimated and terms are often all-consuming, but as long as you work consistently throughout the year there is plenty of time to do extra-curricular activities and go out with friends. There are so many different societies and committees, and having colleges means you can try out sports recreationally at a college level even if you may not want to participate at a University level. It takes a while to get an optimum work-life balance in first term, but most people find that as long as they understand the concepts taught each term, there is plenty of time in the final term to memorise and recap. For Medicine especially, there are heavy contact hours with lectures or practical classes from Monday to Friday often from 9am to 2pm (with a lunch break) or sometimes later until 5pm This may seem daunting, but compared to other degrees at Cambridge, this can often mean less independent studying is needed and you are given most of the resources needed to pass as handouts or debrief sheets.

In terms of the facilities, most of the lectures are in the same cluster of buildings in the centre of the town. There are many libraries in these buildings, and many in other departments and in your college which you have access to – the total number of libraries in the whole University exceeds one hundred. Some prefer coffee shops, spaces around college, or find their room is the best place for no distractions – it is something you have to try out and see what works best, but there are no shortage of options. Each college library can also have useful textbooks to study from; some people use these religiously but this does not always have to be the case and personally I found that online material and the lecture notes were more than enough for me to get through.

A stand out for me in choosing Cambridge was the level of teaching and the collegiate learning set up. Teaching occurs via lectures and practical classes (including the renowned cadaver dissections in first year) and supervisions with other medics from your college. The number of supervisions varies slightly but mostly it is one per week for each module. These usually require some independent revision of the material, and the completion of an essay or set of multiple-choice questions each week, but most supervisors are very friendly and if you are struggling with this for a particular reason they can work out an arrangement to help. The nature of the course means this work can often be done collaboratively with others if you are struggling, although you should make sure that by the end of the supervision you could do it solo as that is how you would be sitting exams. Academically, what you put in is what you get out so some people enjoy spending lots of time in the library doing extra reading and research to get a 1st whilst others do not find this as exciting. Myself and many others in my college did not work as intensively (until exam term) as some of the anecdotes we had heard before coming to Cambridge and still managed to get 1sts and 2:1s – everyone learns differently and comparing hours spent working can often do more harm than good.

What was the application process like?

The application process can seem very daunting - things like entry requirements are often high (A*A*A was typical in my year) and extra tests like the BMAT can be time-consuming. There is no real way around these, so it's important to put in hard work during Y12/13. For interviews, the key thing to remember is to try and not let shyness or nerves get the better of you and to treat it like a practice supervision and prove that you are teachable and enthusiastic. You are definitely not expected to know every answer, but you are expected to have a go at answering questions and think actively, much like a supervision. In this way, it makes sense to have an interview like this as it lets you see how you would fare in the learning environment you are trying to gain entry to.

NATURAL SCIENCES AT CAMBRIDGE

This was contributed by Rachel Tan, a third-year Natural Sciences (biology) student at Newnham College, Cambridge.

How is the course structured?

The course is 3 years long but some subjects have an integrated Masters making it 4 years. The first, second, third and fourth year are called Part IA, IB, II and III. In your first year, you can choose three science subjects and one mathematics subject. There are a wide range of science subjects, from Chemistry to Earth Sciences to Materials Science. Do refer to the website for the full range of subjects. For the mathematical options you also get to choose from Mathematics A or Mathematics B, recommended for those taking Physical Natural Sciences or Mathematical Biology, recommended for those taking Biological Natural Sciences. Of course, these are only recommendations, and there will be someone taking almost any combination of subjects. In your second year, you can choose three subjects from an even larger range of subjects, such as Physiology, Experimental Psychology, and History and Philosophy of Science. Some IB subjects will require that you took the corresponding IA subject e.g Part IB Chemistry A and Part IB Chemistry B will require Part IA Chemistry. Again, many combinations of subjects are possible, and you can choose to focus on a particular area or gain a deeper breadth of knowledge across several fields. In your third year, you can choose to specialise in a particular subject or you can choose one of the two more general courses- Biological and Biomedical Sciences or Physical Sciences. The single subject options will entail a research project comprising approximately 20% of your final grade, while the general course will offer a dissertation instead. Only some subjects will offer a Part III option, which will also comprise a research project.

The assessment for all three years is largely by formal written exams at the end of the academic year, in June. Biological subjects usually will have an essay paper, while physical sciences will comprise several practice questions. The classes are first (1), second-upper (2:1), second-lower class (2:2) and third (3), though in the first year there is no distinction between the second-upper and second-lower class - you will get a second class. Some subjects, especially those of the Physical sciences and Chemistry, will have graded lab reports that are due after every practical. The departments are scattered throughout the city, with the Chemistry department and departments of the Biological sciences are rather centrally located and are quite close to each other. The departments for the Physical sciences are usually located at the West Cambridge site, which is a small cycle away from the city centre. Many department libraries are only accessible to Part II students, but most textbooks you need should be available in the college library or online. Supervisions are held by your college, and since most colleges have quite a large number of Natural Sciences undergraduates, it is not uncommon to be placed in a supervision group only with others from your college, especially in your first year. You will usually have one supervision (lasting one hour) a week per subject. Some subjects also have field courses held during the vacation where you get to travel out of Cambridge and learn more about your subject first-hand.

What is it like to study?

The workload for any course at Cambridge is intense. The Natural Science course is particularly heavy in terms of contact hours, though the number of contact hours decreases after every year. First years will have 12 hours of lectures a week, including Saturday mathematics lectures, while second years have 9 hours of lectures a week. The number of lectures in your third year depends on your particular subject. This is what a typical day in the life of a first-year could look like, though each day is highly varied:

9am – 1pm: Lectures

Lectures are grouped into M/W/F or T/T/S blocks, meaning you will have lectures at that particular time on M/W/F. For example, the Mathematics lectures are 9am every Tuesday, Thursday and Saturday. Lecture notes are usually provided, though they may or may not be printed for you depending on the department. Not all the lectures are recorded (this was pre-Covid, since lectures are online now, they are all pre-recorded and uploaded at a stipulated time), so once COVID measures have been removed, there may be no way of accessing the lecture content unless you attend the lecture. Saturday 9am lectures can be daunting, and many people end up skipping them for extra sleep especially nearing the end of term, but in the end, you should find the study method that suits you best.

11am – 5pm: Labs (can be long or short)

Each subject usually has one or two labs every week or alternate week. If a subject has more than one lab a week, the labs will usually be shorter (e.g two hours from 2pm – 4pm). Your timetable will usually be structured such that your lectures will not clash with your labs, though there are some individuals who had to leave their labs to attend a lecture in between. For subjects with longer labs (11am – 5pm, with a one-hour lunch break in between), labs are usually held only once a week or every two weeks. Additionally, the labs also don't always last till 5pm as it depends on the experiment every week. The content taught in the labs are meant to complement the content you learn in your lectures. There are demonstrators, usually graduate students, assigned to every small group. Don't hesitate to ask them any questions you may have as they are here to help.

5pm – 7pm: Supervisions

As everyone's timetable is slightly different and people have labs on different days, it is common to have supervisions past 5pm (my latest supervision was 7.15pm to 8.15pm). A supervision usually consists of 2-4 students and a supervisor (can be a graduate student, a postdoc or a lecturer). For subjects in the Physical sciences, you will usually be given a problem sheet and you will be assigned some questions to do each week. These questions will build up on content taught in the lectures and are meant to help you reinforce your understanding of the material. For subjects in the Biological sciences, supervisions are more varied. You can be going through essay questions, discussing the content taught in the lectures, or giving presentations on the lecture material. Supervisions are the highlight of Cambridge education, and it allows you to consolidate your understanding of the material and clarify any doubts you have.

Evening: free time

Evenings can be spent either on supervision work or relaxing and having fun. While the course may sound intimidating, there is still time for fun. You can go out with friends, attend formal dinners, or participate in society events. I find that it is important for your mental health to maintain a good work-life balance and not let yourself get overwhelmed with work.

Application process:

The application process usually consists of interviews and the Natural Sciences Admissions Assessment (NSAA) on top of the UCAS application. For the NSAA, I recommend attempting the past year papers to get a feel of what the questions are like. The interviews may seem intimidating, but the key thing is to show the interviewer that you are enthusiastic and teachable. Try to 'think out loud' and have a discussion with the interviewer, and remember that you are definitely not expected to get the answer correct on your first try.

PHILOSOPHY, POLITICS, AND ECONOMICS AT OXFORD

This testimonial is by Jake Robinson, who graduated from PPE at Merton College, Oxford in 2019.

What was the admissions process like?

The admissions process has two main stages, the TSA (sat in November) and the interview (in Oxford, usually in the first half of December). For those that are successful the usual offer is AAA. However, in reality, the vast majority of successful applicants are predicted (and go on to achieve) higher grades and therefore it should be seen as a minimum rather than a target. There are no formal A-Level subject requirements but Maths is advised and, in my experience, far more PPEists have Further Maths than don't have Maths. This does of course depend on route within PPE (discussed later), with Economics requiring a higher degree of Maths than Philosophy or Politics. However, logic in philosophy and elements within politics can benefit from a mathematical mindset.

The TSA is the first hurdle to admission. It is used (alongside grades, references etc.) to decide who to invite to interview. The TSA is very time pressured and this can be quite stressful but after a bit of practice it can become relatively stimulating.

The interview is next and consists of several days in Oxford with 2/3 interviews at your chosen college and the possibility of one at an additional college. The length of the stay can make it quite intense but the interviews take up such a small proportion of the time there that it is a good opportunity to explore Oxford a little and interact with other applicants in the same boat (though be careful of other applicants trying to unnerve you). The interviews themselves can be tough but I found the discussion to be stimulating, after the initial nerves had passed, it is unlike being at school and really gives one a sense of what Oxford and degree level education is about.

How is the course structured?

The PPE course is 3 years long and split into two parts.

First comes prelims (first year), in which you study the basics of all three elements of PPE and there are no optional modules.

For prelims Economics there are three elements: Microeconomics and Macroeconomics which cover basic principles in economics, and Mathematical Techniques which, as the name suggests, focuses on making sure every PPEist has the tools to engage in the study of Economics. Microeconomics and Macroeconomics are taught one per term over two terms through tutorials (usually in college) and lectures (university wide) and assessed through one exam at the end of the year. Mathematical techniques is taught alongside the other two modules and not examined specifically.

For philosophy there are three parts: Logic, Moral philosophy, and General philosophy. These are taught through a combination of classes and tutorials (usually in college), as well as university wide lectures. All three topics are then assessed within one exam paper taken at the end of the year. Each part has a specific flavour, general philosophy introduces students to large questions within philosophy such as Free Will, God, or Identity. Moral philosophy, on the other hand, focuses on introductory ethics (primarily JS Mill and Utilitarianism) whereas logic is an introduction to analytic philosophy and the relationship between logical structures, linguistics, and philosophical arguments.

Prelims Politics consists of three parts too. Firstly, there is The Theory of Politics which covers introductory political theory such as the study of liberty, power, and rights. Secondly is The Practice of Politics which covers questions of political science and in particular comparative government. This covers topics such as empirically assessing the strength of states, role of institutions, or democratization. This is complemented by the Political Analysis module which is an introduction to using quantitative methods (through R) to analyse and answer political questions in a statistical manner. Theory and Practice is examined through one exam at the end of the year whereas Analysis is assessed through an essay in the second term.

Throughout prelims, tutorials for Politics and Philosophy normally require weekly essays whereas Economics require a mixture of problem sheets and essays. This work doesn't form part of the grade you receive in prelims (which is made up from the three exams only) but is still important in its own right. In order to pass prelims, one has to pass each of the three exams, however, these grades don't count towards the overall degree mark. It is also important to note that while there are no optional modules there is choice within modules (in politics and philosophy) meaning that tutors usually accommodate requests to study particular topics within a module (one doesn't study every topic in a module).

After prelims come finals (second and third year) where there is considerably more choice and specialisation. Over these two years eight modules are studied (two a term in second year). At this point it is possible to drop one subject and become Bipartite or carry on with Philosophy, Politics and economics (Tripartite). As eight modules are studied either way it is more common for students to choose Bipartite in order to specialize more, however, a significant minority do keep all three.

Within the eight modules taken there are core and optional modules. For philosophy one has to take Ethics and then either: Early Modern, Aristotle, Plato, or Knowledge and Reality. These largely lead on from Moral and General Philosophy in first year. Then there is a huge range of optional modules ranging from mathematical formal logic to philosophy and everything in between.

For politics one has to pick two of: Comparative government, Theory of Politics, International relations, Political Sociology, and British Political History since 1900. Outside of these there is a huge range of optional modules split along the divide of Practice and Theory as established in Prelims. Therefore one can study, in depth, the politics of particular countries or regions or study particular thinkers or theories.

Finals Economics doesn't have any specific core modules; however, all other modules rely on either Microeconomics or Macroeconomics and therefore in order to select any module one of these has to be taken. Outside of these two a whole range of other modules exists, including development economics, economic history and Welfare economics.

These modules are taught across second and third year, exactly when they are taught depending on various considerations such as when tutors are available, whether other modules have to be taken first etc. All modules are taught in tutorials and classes in a similar manner to first year and are usually held weekly (meaning two tutorials weekly in second year) and each tutorial typically requires an essay. There are also lectures alongside the tutorials. All of the modules are assessed by exam at the end of the third year (no exams in second year!), there is, however, the option to swap a module for a supervised dissertation. The range and diversity of these topics means they are taught by particular tutors around the university rather than within college as is the case in prelims. This also means that you come into contact with a wider range of academics and students than is the case in First Year.

What is it like to study?

The workload is a double-edged sword for PPE. On one hand it can be tough, most weeks contain two essays alongside lectures and other classes. This can entail a lot of time preparing, reading and writing and at times can be stressful. However, unlike some other degrees the structure can be quite freeing, outside of lectures most teaching is on a small scale meaning it can be adjusted to allow time for other activities. Moreover, essays while they require a lot of reading can accommodate flexible working patterns meaning that it is normally possible to find time to do lots of other things.

This means that there is a time to engage in the rich life Oxford has to offer, this can be in the form of sport, music, theatre or one of the millions of societies. Moreover, PPE naturally lends itself to political and debating societies as well as having its own subject society that frequently brings in prominent speakers from across the PPE spectrum.

This freedom in scheduling means it is hard to pin down exactly what a typical day looks like- because people handle it in a range of ways; some work intensely for a shorter time, others are more balanced across the week. However, broadly a first-year week would consist of 1-2 lectures per day, followed by independent reading and research in the afternoons producing essay material for that week's tutorials. Evenings and weekends would contain a little more work but also plenty of time for sports and societies as well as socialising with friends inside and out of college.

There are a huge range of facilities for PPEists, as a degree that incorporates three faculties there are several libraries to choose from, as well as the central Bodleian and college libraries too. This means that material, space and resources are always available when you need them.

Overall one of the key strengths of PPE is its diversity. People come with different interests and different expectations, something that is clear to see when one considers the range of careers PPEists go into. This means that you continually come into contact with people who challenge your perspective and way of thinking and therefore have an opportunity to consider and refine your ideas. This is complemented by the range of topics to study and the range of societies and activities that one can take part in alongside wider study.

PSYCHOLOGY AT OXFORD

This testimonial is by Lewis Webb, who is a graduated in Experimental Psychology from St Edmund Hall, Oxford in 2019.

How is the course structured?

The Experimental Psychology course at Oxford is three years long. In the two terms of year one ('prelims'), your time is split between Introduction to Psychology, Introduction to Neurophysiology and Introduction to Probability Theory and Statistics courses. At the end of the second term, you sit 'prelims' exams. These are made up of three written papers which are marked but not officially graded and do not have any impact on your final degree grade. Year two and three are referred to as Final Honours School (FHS) Part 1 and 2, due to them not coinciding with the academic years.

FHS 1 begins in the third term of year one and runs until the end of term two of year two. You study eight psychology modules in these three terms; social psychology, cognitive neuroscience, developmental psychology, language and cognition, perception, behavioural neuroscience, MAIP (memory, attention and information processing) and PIDPD (personality, individual differences and psychological disorders). In addition to these modules, there are also Core Practicals, which are all assessed via coursework and involve using some of the computer programs (e.g. MATLAP and SPSS) that are taught in the FHS 1 statistics lectures. At the end of term two of year two, you sit five written papers. These are made up of four pairs of psychology subjects and one statistics paper. These papers, along with the Core Practicals coursework, makes up 40% of your final grade.

FHS 2 begins in term three of year two and runs until your final exams. During this time, you study either three advanced options or (like me) two advanced options and a library dissertation. In addition to this, there are Block Practicals, tasks (similar to Core Practicals) which are marked as coursework. You are able to select all aspects of this year's work, with options spanning all previously studied topics, but with more focus. With this in mind, it is important to use prelims and FHS 1 to decide which topics and methods of assessment you prefer! You will also complete a research project during FHS 2. This is an independent piece of work encompassing practical application of knowledge, research practice and writing up a paper. These four sections are equally split (15% each) in weight on your final grade, with the Block Practical results being used as a decider if your final score is on a grade boundary.

What is it like to study?

The workload of this course varies hugely based on what time of year it is, and the topics you select in FHS 2. Prelims is a significant step up from A-Levels, and it is important to treat it as such, in order that your grade can reflect your true ability. This is important for signalling any changes that might need to be made for the section. FHS 1 is the most intense time for exams, the volume of content is enormous and, while much of it is not hugely complex, having perfectly managed notes in advance of the exam period is vital to manage the information. FHS 2 is far more independent than FHS 1, with comparatively few lectures (especially if you opt for the library dissertation instead of a third advanced option). I found it more relaxed than FHS 1, particularly as I made headway with my dissertation and research project during the quiet third term of year two. An Experimental Psychologist's third year is somewhat less intense than most other subjects!

Lectures are typically no more than a few hours a day, with lab time (during FHS) in three-hour blocks once a week. This means that it is important to self-structure your days, as only anywhere from 0-6 hours is likely to be structured for you. The regular task throughout prelims and FHS 1 is essay writing for tutorials, these are typically a couple per week. If you keep on top of these, then there is time for involvement in societies and sporting events, especially throughout prelims and the first two terms of FHS 1. Due to the lessened structure during FHS 2, this is the time that many people choose to give over the most commitment to societies and other interests.

The psychology department building is currently undergoing a huge reconstruction project (and was throughout my entire degree!), so should be very well equipped in a few years' time when complete. Despite this, most other department libraries are accessible by students of different subjects, so work spaces are not limited. Access to psychology books is easy through your college library, or through the social sciences library (SSL). The SSL and the law library are some of the more airy and less intense working environments which is great during the slightly less busy periods! Tutors are also easily contactable and most are very helpful when needing assistance outside of tutorials, this can be vital when coming up to exams!

The Oxford Experience

The Experimental Psychology course is a very science-heavy course and, as a result, so is the research of many of the lecturers and tutors. There are many opportunities to discuss and get involved in some of the latest research in a wide variety of topics. Some of the most accessible are in the baby lab for developmental psychology and studies on cognitive neuroscience and perception. There are a wealth of studies by PhD students and post-doctorate researchers that undergraduates can participate in. This is a requirement during prelims, but is something that can be helpful (not to mention financially rewarding) to continue throughout FHS for insights to improve your own research project.

What was the application process like?

The entry requirements for Experimental Psychology are A*AA at A-Level and, typically, eight A*'s at GCSE. The admissions test is the Thinking Skills Assessment (TSA). This exam includes 50 multiple choice questions testing critical thinking and problem-solving skills and a single essay chosen from some options. The questions are varied in content but many have predictable methods of answering them, so it is important to practice some papers before attempting the real thing! The essay question options typically include some topics that are at the forefront of current news, so be up to date on that!

I had three interviews, which is quite typical; two at my allocated college and one at another. They lasted around half an hour each and encompassed philosophical questioning, data interpretation and discussion of wider reading. The former was to assess whether I might be a better fit for the Psychology and Philosophy course, so don't be thrown off if you get called into a philosophy interview! I would recommend having good knowledge of a select few key psychology-related books, rather than a massive repertoire of titles and summaries. This detail is much of the interview focus, so be prepared for some longer discussions, especially around topics that are of interest to the interviewer! The interviewers can be harsh but they are there to push the limits of your thinking abilities, so don't be put off if only one topic is discussed throughout an interview.

PSYCHOLOGY AT CAMBRIDGE

This testimonial is by Lucy Pilling, who is a 2nd year in Psychological and Behavioral Sciences at Jesus College, Cambridge.

How is the course structured?

Psychology at Cambridge is titled Psychological and Behavioural Sciences, a three year degree. This course gives you unique flexibility over what you study, able to choose modules from multiple other degrees. The course is structured the same in first and second year: there are two core modules whereas the other two are optional, choosing from an array of other degrees. In first year the core modules are PBS1 and PBS2. PBS1 is a broad introduction to theoretical and methodological processes in psychology, covering a new interesting topic every week such as; personality, gender, intelligence and emotions. PBS2 covers the basic biology of the brain, statistics and research methods. In second year PBS3 and PBS4 are the core options. PBS3 covers developmental and social psychology in detail whereas PBS4 is a shared module with natural sciences studying neurobiology of the brain. In both years optional modules can primarily be taken from; the Natural Sciences Tripos, Human Social and Political Sciences, Philosophy and then Biological Anthropology. In third year you do a dissertation which is an interesting research project with staff in the department, as well as taking one psychology module from a number of options, and a further two module that may be selected from the psychology department or a similarly broad array of areas as in first and second year. I have taken biological anthropology modules in both first and second year and they are my favourite by far, I plan on taking some in third year as well. The BioAnth course covers really interesting content on how humans evolved and why we may have certain social and intellectual traits based on the ecology of the environments our cultures evolved in. I find it really interesting to consider how this may be seen in the more purely psychology topics we study!

The course is assessed by a 3-hour exam per module at the end of each year, although this can differ slightly for optional modules. Unlike some Universities where grades over multiple years are compounded into a final grade, we are given an overall grade at the end of each year based on that year's exams, meaning that the grade used for employers is usually just your third year grade. Many students see this as an advantage as it means that you have been able to build up a substantial toolkit over your three years at Cambridge by the time you take the exams that contribute to this final grade.

What is it like to study?

The workload is high, however, it is definitely manageable and all the content is very interesting which helps too. Because the optional modules are taken from different courses the workload is quite decentralised meaning it can clump up into busier and quieter periods, lots of planning can help make this a more even spread.

A typical week has 8 hours of lectures, two per module, all before lunch and then 2-4 hours of labs a week for PBS2/PBS4. This is alongside 2-3 supervisions a week which are sessions with an expert in the field in groups of 1-3. Supervisions are the most unique feature of learning at Cambridge, they really help to expand knowledge giving deeper insight and making you consider alternate perspectives, whilst deeply consolidating understanding and allowing you to ask any questions you may have.

For each supervision you are usually required to do further reading and write an essay, this is the bulk of the work you are set but it quickly becomes a very manageable routine. I typically take 2-3 days to read and consolidate lecture notes and then a day to write the essay, however, I am known for a rather intense working style of a few stressful days and then a few days off! It is actually really easy to get everything done as long as you plan in advance, and supervisors are always understanding about extensions if your work is too clumped. By consolidating working hours into smart bursts I have loads of spare time to relax with friends, participate in college sports and societies! I play in the college netball team, go to art club, volunteer and take part in marketing or consulting work experience schemes.

There are great facilities all around the city, all colleges have amazing libraries as do departments and the university library is huge and grand, it acquires a copy of every book published in the UK.

For me a typical day usually consists of 1-2 hours of lectures in the morning, I usually try and do an hour or two of work in and around these before returning home for lunch with my friends. I will then likely spend another hour or two working before a supervision in the afternoon. The rest of my afternoon may consist of meeting up with friends or exercising before possibly a little more work. In the evenings I like to cook and relax with a large group of friends. Every day is so busy, but it makes me feel like I am living life to the max!

What was the application process like?

At Cambridge you apply to your course through the colleges, most colleges require A*AA although some require A*A*A. Additionally most colleges may requires maths or biology A level, though this does vary so be sure to look into each college.

Applying to Cambridge can be a daunting prospect but it is very manageable if you prepare well! You of course must write a personal statement, then fill in Cambridge's SAQ which is just further information on your educational experience. For PBS there is a 3-part admission test you sit in November. First there are thinking skills comprehension questions. This is followed by a choice between either a biology and maths multiple choice section or an English multiple choice section. Finally you must write an essay on an obscure title, trying to incorporate psychological knowledge. Practising all of this really helps! Finally if you are successful you will be invited to interview, at my College this consisted of two 20 minute interviews that covered why I wanted to apply for PBS, thought provoking psychology based questions, reactions to data and then questions related more specifically to the books on my personal statement.

VETERINARY MEDICINE AT CAMBRIDGE

This article was contributed by Rebecca Illingworth, a tutor with UniAdmissions, and a Sixth year in Veterinary Medicine at Newnham College.

Veterinary Medicine at Cambridge is a six-year course, the first three years are preclinical and the second three years are clinical. During the preclinical years you will have a similar experience to lots of other students. There are lectures and practicals in the centre town (very convenient!) and trips to the university farm and animal husbandry college for practical animal handling experience. Over the preclinical years you will also have supervisions which involve 2-4 students and a supervisor discussing a recent lecture topic for an hour. The clinical years are a brilliant mixture of lectures and practicals in Veterinary Department (only a 15-minute cycle from town) and rotations, where you get to start treating animals and developing the practical skills you need to be a vet.

First year has three main modules: Anatomy, Physiology and Biochemistry, each with 3 exams in May/June, and two minor modules of Epidemiology and Animal husbandry, each with one exam in March. Anatomy is made up of 3 lectures a week and 2 dissections classes, where you are split into groups of four and each group is given a dog cadaver to dissect throughout the year, these sessions are great fun and really help you develop practical anatomical knowledge. Physiology had a similar structure to Anatomy with 3 lectures a week and 1-2 practicals. Biochemistry also has 3 lectures a week but instead has just one practical a term which lasts most of the day. In first year you also spend one afternoon a week rotating through different animal handling practicals, getting hands on experience handling pigs, horses, sheep, exotics and more.

THE ULTIMATE OXBRIDGE COLLEGE GUIDE — DEGREE PROFILES

Second year has five main modules: Neuroanatomy & physiology, Pharmacology, Pathology, Reproductive anatomy & physiology, and Comparative vertebrate anatomy, examined in May/June and one minor module: Preparing for the veterinary profession, examined in March. Each week you have between 8-13 lectures and 2-4 practicals a week, these practicals are a mixture of dissection and lab-based work. This year has a similar structure to first year but with more modules it is slightly more intense. Over first and second year you have weekly supervisions for all the main modules and less frequent supervisions for the other modules, these are your opportunities to ask any questions you have and really aid in your understanding of the subject.

In third year you choose a Natural Sciences to study. Options include Biochemistry, Genetics, Neuroscience, Physiology, Pathology, Psychology, Zoology etc. The structure of the year is different depending on which modules you choose, but in general you will study 3-5 modules of your choice. For example, in Zoology you choose 4-5 modules out of 20 options, which allows you to choose what really interests you. You also choose between completing a research project or 6,000-word dissertation on a related subject of your choice. At the end of the year you graduate with a BA in Natural Sciences, allowing you to celebrate with all your undergraduate friends on different courses who are graduating "for real".

Fourth and fifth year are made up of several modules, with a mixture of species-based and systems approaches, for example: Cattle Medicine, Exotics Medicine, Soft Tissue Surgery, Principles of Oncology, Dermatology etc. Alongside lectures and practicals and you have "Small Group Clinical Practicals" two mornings a week where you develop practical skills, including how to: do a neurological exam, correctively trim cattle feet, examine dogs' eyes, rectal examination of pregnant cows, etc. One practical is at the RSPCA clinic, where you will first see your own patients, starting with vaccination clinics to gain confidence you progress on to taking full histories, discussing treatment plans with the vets in charge and explaining these plans to the owners. In fifth year you also do "treatments", where you spend a week in pairs helping administer medications to the patients in the hospital. There are 1-3 exams at the end of each term over these two years.

Sixth year is a lecture free year, you have 22-weeks of rotations in a 40-week period. All these rotations involve working with a different team within the equine, farm and small animal hospitals; helping to treat patients, discussing cases in detail, and communicating with clients. These rotations include: Radiology (you learn to take x-rays), soft tissue surgery (you scrub into surgery and assist), equine ambulatory, farm animal production (lots of practice rectalling), anaesthesia, etc. The weeks off in between rotations give you good opportunity to compete EMS placements at veterinary practices of your choosing (you need to do 26 weeks of these over the three clinical years). After finals (4 exams & vivas in May) you graduate and become a vet.

What is it like to study?

The workload at Cambridge, specifically Veterinary Medicine, should not be underestimated, however, it is definitely manageable especially if you passionate about the subject. You have incredibly busy 8-week terms in the first 3 years and then steadier 10-week terms in fourth and fifth year and sixth year is more similar to working, where you are busy for longer hours during the day but need to do a lots less self-directed work once you go home. This may seem like a lot of work but there is plenty of time for other activities. I was able to play sport throughout these busy terms, playing university Basketball and rowing for my college, and most vet students have similar commitments to extracurriculars, so there is the time and opportunity to have a diverse university experience.

The Cambridge Experience

One great thing about studying Veterinary Medicine at Cambridge is the small year size, there are only 60-75 students per year group, so you get to know all the vets in your year and many in other years too, it is an incredibly supportive tight-knit community. Supervisions are an incredibly helpful advantage to studying in Cambridge, they give you many opportunities to ask questions about anything you are struggling with. Living in picturesque colleges for the first 3 years, as most students do, is a truly unique experience and allows you to make friends doing other subjects as well as those on your course. College formal dinners are another great bonus of Cambridge, you dress up and wear gowns to have a delicious (and subsidised!) 3-course meal. In the later years most students live with other vets, often with their dissection group from first year, normally still within walking distance from town. Unlike other veterinary schools, everything in Cambridge is really close together, you rarely have to cycle more than 15-minutes to get anywhere over all 6 years, this is incredibly convenient and really adds to the community feel you get whilst studying in Cambridge.

What was the application process like?

After applying through UCAS you fill out the SAQ (Supplementary Application Questionnaire) which asks a few additional questions about your motivation for studying VetMed at Cambridge and more in-depth detail on your previous exams results. Interviews take place in early December and you will have between 2-3 interviews in your chosen college, these are almost always on the same day and accommodation is provided to students who need it. All my interviewers were friendly and when I did not know answers they give you clues to help you get to the answer, so it was less daunting than I expected. Offers are made in January, you will either receive an offer from your chosen college or you may be "pooled" to another college and receive your offer from them. The Veterinary offer is A*AA, you must be taking Chemistry and one of Biology, Physics or Maths. Students taking four A-levels are often given A*AAA offers, so this is worth keeping in mind when deciding how many A levels to take. In February there is an offer holder day, where you learn more about the course, get a tour of the vet school and meet your future year group.

Closing Words

Hopefully these accounts have been valuable to you while you think about which subjects you'd like to apply for. If you are interested in a subject which hasn't been covered here, contact us through the website at www.uniadmissions.co.uk and we'll be happy to arrange a casual chat with current students on any Oxford or Cambridge course!

Below is our guide to the Oxbridge and Cambridge colleges, which should be your next step when thinking about applying to Oxbridge.

CAMBRIDGE COLLEGES

There are 31 different colleges at Cambridge, which we've arranged in alphabetical order across the following pages.

All of the information here was contributed by current and recent students of these colleges, so it should be all be up to date, with the possible exception of the bar prices! You'll be able to find great detail on all the colleges on their respective websites, in particular the student union sites. Each Cambridge college has two student unions, known as common rooms – there is normally a literal common room, hence the name – one for undergraduate, and one for graduate students. They should both have their own websites, which will provide far more detail than we were able to here.

Our goal was to provide all this information in one place, easily arranged for you to flick through and see which colleges you're interested in learning more about. We'd like to thank all of the following students who helped with these profiles, which were by far the hardest part of the book to write, so thank you to:

- Ana Leonescu
- Arabella Zuckerman
- Benjamin Remez
- Camille Gontarek
- Emma Jackson
- Fiona McNally
- Ishan Jain
- Jemima Becker
- Lizzy Cole
- Lucy Pilling
- Riana Patel

Christ's College

Founded: 1505

Famous Alumni: Charles Darwin, John Milton, Sacha Baron Cohen

Undergraduates: ~450   **Postgraduates:** ~170

Accommodation: Student accommodation throughout college. Modern typewriter at the back of the college with cheap rooms for first years, medium priced rooms for third years in third court and expensive sixteenth century rooms in second and first court for scholars.

Bar: Buttery in First court Price of a Pint: £3.00

Chapel & Religion: Christian

College Payment System: Cash

Food: Upper hall- café style (breakfast lunch dinner) or formal hall (dinner 6 times a week)

Formality: Gowns to be worn at formal hall dinners, chapel services and graduation

Grants and Bursaries: Grants for travel, academic endeavours. Bursaries for hardship reasons

Location: Very central. Close to shopping centres, many libraries and science campuses

Politics & Reputation: Known for being very academic, often tops Tompkins table

Sport: Very near to its boat club on the river. Has hockey, netball, football, badminton, rugby, volleyball, cricket, swimming, water polo and more college teams.

ULTIMATE OXBRIDGE COLLEGE GUIDE | CAMBRIDGE COLLEGES

Churchill College

Founded: 1958

Famous Alumni: Sir John Stuttard (Former Mayor of London), Bjarne Stroustrup (Inventor of C++), Kari Blackburn (BBC World Service executive)

Undergraduates: ~450   **Postgraduates:** ~280

Accommodation: A variation of rooms, all with a large window seat. En-suites are available. Cowan Court was recently built and has modern style rooms which all have double beds and en-suites for ~ £1800. Cheaper rooms are available with a single bed and communal bathroom.

Bar: There is a bar in the buttery with a large range of food and drinks Price of a Pint: £4

Chapel & Religion: There is a chapel at the end of the college grounds. However, as a mainly scientific college, the chapel plays a small role in the college.

College Payment System: There is a direct debit transfer at the end of every term where accommodation and any food bought using your student card (e.g. dinner in hall) is paid for.

Food: Lunch and dinner are served every day in hall. There are usually 2 or 3 vegetarian/vegan options as well as meat options and a salad bar. Students can pay on their student cards. The chefs in the kitchen are happy to listen to food requests from students so that everyone can eat well.

Formality: Churchill is regarded as the least formal college, being the only college where gowns are not required for formal hall. The college also takes the highest proportion of state school students in general.

Grants and Bursaries: There is a new bursary funded by Amazon for female computer scientists at Churchill. There are also music bursaries and bursaries for students from low-income households (less than £42,620 pa). There are also grants for current students for music lessons, playing sports and vacation travel/courses.

Location: It is located Storey's Way, next to Murray Edwards College and Fitzwilliam College. It is a 20-minute walk from town or a 5/10-minute cycle. As it is not as central as other colleges, it is useful to be able to cycle.

Politics & Reputation: Churchill a reputation of being mainly for STEM subjects although humanities students are encouraged to apply. The motto is forward as the college endeavours to be forward thinking.

Sport: Churchill has playing fields on site, unlike many other colleges. There are football pitches, a cricket pitch, a rugby pitch, tennis courts, squash courts and a gym. The football club are in League 1 and were the first college team to retain the League division 1 title. There is also a very successful boat club for rowers.

Clare College

Founded: 1326

Famous Alumni: Kwame Anthony Appiah, Henry Louis Gates Jr., John Rutter, and Sir David Attenborough!

Undergraduates: ~500   **Postgraduates:** ~270

Accommodation: All the first years live in Memorial Court on Queens' Road, which has a variety of rooms at different costs to suit different budgets. After first year, accommodation is allocated by lottery, so each student is allocated a number in the ballot for second year, which is then reversed for third year. Bad room in second year= Good room in third year.

Second years all live in Clare College Colony on Chesterton Lane, which also has a range of room prices to suit different budgets and has the option for students to ballot to live together in friendship groups. This is the same for third year, although some third years are lucky enough to live in Old Court, maybe even overlooking the river.

Bar: Clare has the best bar in Cambridge (probably) in the crypt underneath the chapel, known as Clare Cellars. All the other colleges are jealous of how good it is!

Price of a Pint: £3.20

Chapel & Religion: Clare is also known for its fantastic music society and famous chapel choir!

College Payment System: There is a direct debit transfer at the end of every term where accommodation and any food bought using your student card (e.g. dinner in hall) is paid for.

Food: Clare has come first in many inter-collegiate catering competitions, meaning our formal is excellent and well-priced- Around £7.50 for Clare students. Our buttery is less consistently good, although it can surprise you. Clare has a lot of vegetarian and vegan students, so is good at catering for them, and will cater for other dietary requirements as long as they know in advance. Every student will have access to a gyp room (small kitchen) with a toaster, microwave and two-ring hob- This is better than it sounds! Ovens are a rarity for undergraduates.

Formality: Clare is one of the older colleges, but while some aspects are quite formal, it's a very relaxed vibe. It's not a competitive place academically, so it doesn't feel as intense as some other colleges can.

Location: Clare is right in the centre of town, overlooking the river and the backs. Some of the accommodation is a little further out though, so there is some travel involved.

Sport: There are lots of sports societies to get involved in at college level. This is very relaxed, social and the levels of ability are not as high as the university teams! In particular Clare has a big boat club, so many people give rowing a go, even if the early start in the winter mean that some don't stick with it!

Clare Hall

Founded: 1966

Famous Alumni: Seamus Heaney was a fellow – as a new college, not many yet, but maybe you one day!

Undergraduates: ~0   **Postgraduates:** ~145

Bar: A new bar, the Anthony Lowe building, has just opened, which is very exciting, and an increasingly popular venue for grad student from other colleges. We have a party almost every Saturday in term time.

Price of a Pint: £3.90

Formality: Clare Hall is one of the least formal colleges. There aren't any undergrads, so fellows and student mix freely without high table or gowns. If you didn't know, you'd not be able to tell who was a professor and who a student!

Location: Clare Hall is in West Cambridge, near the University Library, but a good fifteen minutes' walk to the shops in town. The bus does stop right outside though, if you don't fancy cycling!

Sport: Clare Hall boasts a multigym, heated indoor swimming pool – much nicer than the unheated outdoor one at Emmanuel – and tennis court at the West Court site, just a little way down Herschel Road. Sport at Clare Hall has really taken off over the past few years, and now we have very active running, football, cricket, yoga and boat clubs.

Corpus Christi College

Founded: 1352

Famous Alumni: Christopher Marlowe, Robert Greene, Christopher Isherwood, Helen Oyeyemi, and Kevin McCloud

Undergraduates: ~250 **Postgraduates:** ~200

Accommodation: Accommodation in Corpus is really good and living so close to the main college facilities like Hall, the library, the bar and common room is really handy. Buildings vary from very modern and recently renovated to traditional and historic.

First years are grouped together, either on the main college site or on the streets just either side of it, meaning they live not more than two minute walks from college. Second and third years get to choose where they want to live through a ballot system, with an order decided by names drawn from a hat (the order in second year is reversed for third year).

Third years pick their rooms first, normally choosing to live on the main college site in New Court or Old Court (some of the oldest university accommodation in the world!) while second years normally choose to live in buildings slightly further from the main site, but still only eight minutes walk away.

Food: Catered food in Corpus is generally regarded as really good - with Saturday 'brunch' being a particular college favourite. The regular menu manages to be pretty diverse, with four main courses on offer at lunch, and three at dinner - plus various soups, sides and salads. This includes at least one veggie option, and pescatarians normally have a seafood/fish option at lunch too. Other dietary requirements are catered for at Formal Hall (optional twice-weekly, three-course dinners which happen in addition to normal meals), but are not guaranteed normally.

Grants and Bursaries: The college is really financially supportive with rent support, book grants, and support with living costs. The college is one of the richest in Cambridge, considering its size, so will make sure that you don't have to worry about money if you're having difficulties.

Location: Right in the centre of town, opposite the scary clock! Corpus is well hidden away, but it's bigger than it looks on the outside.

Sport: For a small college, Corpus punches above its weight in regards to sports. Lacrosse, netball, rugby, rowing, tennis, football, and frisbee are just a few on offer. Although usually quite successful, these teams really are open to all abilities - as is the annual 'Corpus Challenge', where we go head-to-head with Corpus Christi Oxford in various sports (and we usually win).

Darwin College

Founded: 1958

Famous Alumni: Jane Goodall, Nigel Warburton, Elizabeth Blackburn

Undergraduates: ~0 **Postgraduates:** ~650

Accommodation: Good, but quite expensive, as the college doesn't subsidise it as much as some of the older colleges, although since we're a grad only college, it's normal for people to live off site.

Formality: Darwin was the first grad only college and is one of the least formal colleges.

Location: Darwin is just over the river, next to the water meadows and the punting station. It is also having its own island, where you can have a BBQ!

Downing College

Founded: 1800

Famous Alumni: John Cleese, Thandie Newton, Michael Winner

Undergraduates: ~400   **Postgraduates:** ~250

Accommodation: Accommodation at Downing has a reputation for being amazing! For first years, you'll be asked to indicate what price band room you want, and will be allocated a room that way. There are 4 accommodation blocks and 1 staircase in college only for freshers, which is a great way to get to know everyone. Lots of first year rooms have double beds and en-suites!

Second- and third-year accommodation are allocated by a random ballot, which you can enter as a group of friends. You pick your room (either a room in college staircases, or a room in one of the houses on Lensfield Road) according to your order in the ballot. The ballot order is reversed for third year, so if you were last in the ballot in second year, you still get a good pick!

Food: Food at Downing is a highlight! Lots of people go to Hall to eat (people call it 'slops', but this is definitely not a reflection of the quality of the food!), which is a great time to catch up with people over lunch or dinner. Hall does lunch and dinner every weekday, with hot food and a salad bar always available. At the weekends, brunch and dinner are served. At each meal, there is always a vegetarian option available, and sometimes vegan options. The Butterfield Cafe in college serves food for breakfast (croissants, bacon rolls etc.), and also does sandwiches, baguettes, paninis and salads throughout the day. Formal hall (optional) runs 3 times a week, where students and fellows are served a 3 course meal, can bring wine and wearing formal dress and gowns is compulsory. Vegetarian, vegan and nearly all other dietary requirements are always catered for. Formal hall is a great way to wind down or celebrate someone's birthday!

College provides lots of food, but there is also the option to cook in your accommodation. Most Freshers' accommodation has well-equipped kitchens, with hobs, ovens and fridge-freezers, which is unusual for Cambridge. Some of the larger accommodation blocks, as well as the houses on Lensfield Road for second and third years, have large dining tables and much bigger kitchens - perfect for eating together with your housemates.

Location: You could easily walk right past Downing, as it's just a gate off of the main road as you come into town from the train station. We have the biggest open green space though, so it's lovely once you get in and look around!

Sport: Downing has a reputation for being good at sports, with strong teams in nearly every sport. A classic Cambridge sport to get involved in is rowing, but there's everything else from football to frisbee to get involved with.

Emmanuel College

Founded: 1958

Famous Alumni: John Harvard (founder of Harvard University), Jonathan Swift, Richard Attenborough, Lemuel Gulliver (fictionally)

Undergraduates: ~500   **Postgraduates:** ~130

Accommodation: In first year, everyone is allotted rooms in either North Court or South Court. You indicate a preference before arriving - the rooms are all lovely, and are priced according to a grading system (1-8, with 1 being the cheapest and 8 the most expensive). All fresher accommodation is Grade 3-5. In second year, there's a ballot system, and those whose names are drawn first get first pick of rooms. There are options to live out of college. In third year, the ballot gets reversed, so those at the top in second year are at the bottom in third year. Third year rooms are the nicest - notably, there's Old Court, a 17th century building with lots of sets of rooms that you share with a friend. All accommodation in Emmanuel (Emma) is great, there's lots of variety and choice, and everyone always ends up being really happy with where they live! There's also accommodation for grad students in their first year.

Bar: There is a bar in south court, is one of the only student run bars left in Cambridge, and so has some of the cheapest prices as well. There's a twice termly bar extension when it stays open until 2am as well.

Price of a Pint: £2.20

Chapel & Religion: The dean is one of the nicest in Cambridge famous for defying the ban on blessing same sex partnerships nearly twenty years ago! The choir is well regarded and goes on regular tours around Europe and to America.

College Payment System: There is a direct debit transfer at the end of every term where accommodation and any food bought using your student card (e.g. dinner in hall) is paid for. It's paid for as part of your college bill at the end of term, so you never need to worry about running out of credit.

Food: The food in college is usually good. We have a cafeteria which serves a range of hot meals and sandwiches for lunch and dinner with cereals and cooked breakfast every day in the morning. There is always a vegetarian option but it can be a little repetitive. There are vegan sandwiches available but not always a hot option. Most people's favourite meal of the week is Sunday brunch which offers a full cooked breakfast, cereal and some 'lunch-type' hot dishes. Most evenings formal hall takes place at 7.30. This is a three-course meal served in the dining hall which students can book themselves in for, it is popular for events such as birthdays. The food at formal hall is really good and any dietary requirements can be catered for.

Formality: Emma is fairly formal – gowns for formal hall, Latin Grace and a high table. That said, you can walk on almost all of the grass, and there is an outdoor swimming pool, so it's hard to be formal in your swimming costume!

Location: It is located in the centre of town, just opposite the shopping centre. The gates and portico look quite off-putting, so we don't get many tourists, which can be annoying at some of the older colleges.

Fitzwilliam College

Founded: Began in 1869 as a non-collegiate institution, became a college in 1966.

Famous Alumni: David Starkey (Historian and television presenter), Vince Cable (Politician) and Cressida Dick (Commissioner of the Metropolitan Police)

Undergraduates: ~500   **Postgraduates:** ~400

Accommodation: For undergraduates, first years live on the main college site in newly-refurbished modern rooms with showers and washbasins. There are shared kitchen and bathroom facilities. Second, third and fourth years also mainly live on the college site. However, half of second years live in nearby college-owned houses. Undergraduate rents in the 2018-19 year ranged from £108-£169.50 a week. Fitzwilliam is usually able to provide a single room to all postgraduates, on the main site or in college houses. Double rooms and flats are also available but more competitive to get.

Bar: Fitz Bar is open every night and offers a wide range of drinks including the "Fitz Lager". The bar hosts events such as discos (bops) and quizzes during term-time. Price of a Pint: £2.40 - £3.30

Chapel & Religion: The chapel is open to students of all and no faiths. It is also home of the Christian Union and offers a weekly main service during term-time. The chaplain also runs welfare events, such as drinks receptions, walks and cake breaks during term.

College Payment System: You use your CamCard to pay for food and printing. Cash and card can also be used at some facilities. You buy tokens from the Café to use in the laundry facilities. Transactions made on your CamCard, along with college bills, can be paid for by direct debit on an online system.

Food: Fitz provides a lunch and dinner service in the main hall every day. Currently, lunch on a Saturday and Sunday is a full-English breakfast, and dinner on a Tuesday is a special theme-night meal. Optional formal gowned dinners are also served on Wednesdays and Fridays after the main dinner service. The bar turns into a café during the day and offers light snacks such as paninis, sandwiches and cakes.

Formality: Fitz is a modern college, as reflected by its students, architecture, library and gardens, so would be regarded as one of the least formal colleges.

Grants and Bursaries: A full list of bursaries available to Fitz students can be found on the Fitz website. Students are emailed termly about what financial support is available by the college. Prizes are also currently available for students achieving first-class examination grades during their time at Fitz.

Location: Fitz is deemed a 'hill college' due to it being slightly out of town. However, it takes roughly 20 minutes to walk and 10 minutes to cycle to town for lectures, so the distance should not deter you from applying.

Politics & Reputation: Fitz is often regarded as a very friendly college, with students and staff that are welcoming and forward-thinking. Fitz also has an excellent reputation for outreach, which stems from its history of being an institution to allow students who could not afford college membership to access Cambridge. Fitz's motto is "the best of the old and the new", reflecting its modern atmosphere. A Fitz student is called a 'Fitzbilly' in honour of the billy goat that serves as the college mascot.

Sport: Fitz has around 20 sports clubs, with a particularly successful football and cricket team. The college site has a gym free to college members, squash and badminton courts, and currently runs free Yoga sessions for students.

Girton College

Founded: 1869

Famous Alumni: Dina bint 'Abdu'l-Hamid; Margrethe II, of Denmark; Hisako, Princess Takamado; Sandi Toksvig; Arianna Huffington; Karen Spärck Jones; Rachel Lomax; Mary Arden; Gwyneth Lewis; Brenda Hale, Baroness Hale of Richmond; Bertha Swirles

Undergraduates: ~500 **Postgraduates:** ~220

Accommodation: The college can accommodate all students for all their years of study, and there are standard and en-suite rooms. There is a choice of rooms in the main College building, Ash Court, Swirles Court or in a College-owned house, including Family Accommodation. Rent: £172.50 per week (standard room); £180.50 per week (en-suite room)

Bar: Both the Social Hub and Bar are available for socialising and events

Price of a Pint: £2.20

Chapel & Religion: The Chapel is a community and a haven for all College members, playing an important and diverse role in College life – for those of all faiths and of none

College Payment System: The college bill is paid at the beginning of each term. Our college student card is used for purchasing food and drinks from the Cafeteria and Social Hub, and the amount is then added to the college bill.

Food: Breakfast, lunch and dinner are available in the Cafeteria Mon-Fri, as well as brunch and dinner at the weekends, at reasonable prices. There is a variety of options, including meat, fish and veg options every day. Snacks are also available both in the Cafeteria and Social Hub. Girton students can also get food for student price at some town colleges (Downing and Robinson), for those whose departments are central.

Formality: In general, pretty chilled. Gowns are required at formal hall though, and you're not allowed in the dining hall in your pyjamas!

Grants and Bursaries: Bursaries and hardship funds are available to eligible individuals. Girton has a fund to make small contributions to academic-related expenses. You must be an Undergraduate or Clinical Medic or Vet at the time of the expenditure to be eligible to apply. The College has a fund to make small contributions to sport-related expenses. Girton gives 35-40 Travel Awards each year to its undergraduate students. Graduate scholarships and studentships are available for post-graduate students who put Girton as their first or second choice.

Location: Girton has the reputation of being the far-away college in Cambridge. Girton village is technically separate from Cambridge. Cambridge is a small city though, so Girton is only 15-20 minutes cycling to the centre of town!

Politics & Reputation: As the first college in Cambridge that would admit women, the college takes pride in its founding values of inclusion, equality and diversity.

Sport: Girton's main site has the best on-site sports facilities of any Cambridge college. There are full-size well-maintained football, rugby, and cricket pitches. Hard courts for basketball, netball and tennis are also available. Inside, there is a squash court and multi-gym equipped with free weights and a range of other equipment. Girton is the only college to have its own heated indoor swimming pool. There is a great variety of college sports clubs and teams, for all abilities!

Gonville and Caius College

Founded: 1348

Famous Alumni: William Harvey, Stephen Hawking, Francis Crick & James Watson, James Chadwick, Howard Florey

Undergraduates: ~500   **Postgraduates:** ~250

Accommodation: One of the best in Cambridge for undergraduates. First years live in the Stephen Hawking Building or Harvey Court which are newly refurbished buildings with gyms, table tennis tables and common rooms. Most people will live in college in their third year which is centrally located, full of character and generally quite spacious. The huge downside is that the college operates a 'no-hobs' policy which severely restricts the variety of food that you can cook. The kitchens will still have microwaves, kettles and George Foreman grills though.

Bar: Run by college staff and located in the heart of college below the hall. This is a great place to relax after a formal dinner and unwind with friends.

Price of a Pint: Around £2.50

Chapel & Religion: Caius is a tradition-filled college. The college chapel choir has performed live on national radio and is very competitive to get into. Caius is one of the colleges to allow students/alumni to get married in college which always makes for a great wedding setting.

Food: Very hit and miss. Caius has a reputation for serving poor food but this has dramatically improved of late. Formal hall takes place six nights per week where students are required to wear gowns, Grace is read out loud and a three-course silver-service dinner follows. Normally, most students don't dress 'formally' as it happens so frequently. You can also attend an informal hall every night (no Grace, identical food and service). You reserve the halls through an online portal and each meal costs around £7. Unfortunately, you are forced to buy 40+ tickets every term (and are charged for this, even if you don't attend hall). As a result of this, and the lack of hobs, most students attend hall at least five times per week.

Formality: Caius is immersed in tradition. Students must obtain 'terminal exeats' before leaving college for holidays and Grace is said before every formal hall as examples.

Grants and Bursaries: Caius is one of the wealthiest colleges in Cambridge and has lots of grants available for students. There are many travel grants available (up to £2000) as well as a books grant (£50 per year). Students from a disadvantaged background are also entitled to further bursaries.

Location: Centrally located and a short 3-minute walk to the Sainsbury's where students spend a large portion of their shopping time. It's a 5-10 minute cycle to pretty much every lecture hall, lab or sports facility.

Politics & Reputation: Caius is renowned for being the best place to study medicine in the world and has very strong medical roots with William Harvey (circulatory system) as well as Waston & Crick (DNA). The college accepts the most medical applicants out of any Oxbridge college and students are provided with top-tier teaching. Many of the supervisors are senior examiners and run their own labs which provide research-keen scientists a perfect stepping stone to academia. The college library is also one of the best in the university.

Sport: Very strongly funded rowing club – the boat club gets a huge proportion of the student budget and hence has top-tier equipment including Olympic level boats! As Caius is a large college, most sports are well represented including badminton, football, table tennis, rugby. It's a safe bet that there will be a society for you to join here.

Fun Fact: It's pronounced Gonville and 'Keys' – don't say 'Kai-us', the taxi drivers won't know where you mean!

Homerton College

Founded: 1768 and became a full College of the University in 2010

Famous Alumni: Olivia Coleman, Nick Hancock, Leah Manning, Sam Yates

Undergraduates: ~600   **Postgraduates:** ~800

Accommodation: Homerton College has several different accommodation blocks and the majority of the rooms are en-suite. In first year everyone is guaranteed an en-suite bedroom. The accommodation is very reasonably priced and is one of the cheapest amongst the Cambridge Colleges. Each accommodation block also has several gyps (little kitchens), usually shared between 8 or 9 people. Each gyp has a fridge, hobs, a microwave, a kettle and a sink and everyone has their own cupboard. Every undergraduate student is guaranteed accommodation in college for all years of their undergraduate degree.

Bar: Homerton is lucky to have two different bars. One is called The Griff and functions only as a bar and the other is the College Buttery which also doubles up as a bar in the evenings. Both are very good places to socialise. Price of a Pint: £2-3

Chapel & Religion: Homerton doesn't have a College Chapel however there is a Prayer Room which students can use.

College Payment System: The College uses a system called 'UPAY' and each student uses their CamCard (University ID) to pay for their food. You can also use a bank card to pay for food but the CamCard gives students a discounted price.

Food: The College offers breakfast, lunch and dinner from Monday to Friday and runs brunch on the weekend. The food is very reasonably priced and caters for vegetarians and vegans. There are normally 3 or 4 main meal options and 3 or 4 options for sides as well as a salad bar. The College also has a Buttery (café) where students can buy sandwiches, salads, cakes, snacks, hot drinks and smoothies.

Formality: The College hosts a formal dinner (known as 'Formal Hall') once a week on a Tuesday evening where dinner is served by candlelight with wine. Grace is sung by the choir before each formal. Gowns are optional at Homerton formals. There are several themed formals throughout the year including Harry Potter and the Mad Hatter's Tea Party.

Grants and Bursaries: While Cambridge offers various bursaries as a University, Homerton also offers hardship support as a College to those with particular needs. There are Hardship Grants, Vacation Study Grants (for those who wish to remain in Cambridge during the holidays), an Internship Scholarship, other funds for unexpected hardships, small grants for Academic Projects, the Pilkington Travel Award and also Language Centre reimbursement for those who wish to learn or keep up a language alongside their degree. More details can be found on the College website. (www.homerton.cam.ac.uk)

Location: Homerton is a little further out from the centre of Cambridge and is located between Cambridge Train Station and Addenbrooke's Hospital. There are regular buses which run into town at £1 for a single and it takes around 10-15 minutes to cycle into town or to Sidgwick Site.

Politics & Reputation: Homerton College has a great reputation amongst the Cambridge Colleges and was voted 'Cambridge's Friendliest College'. It is known for being a caring and fun College which prides itself on its student community.

Sport: Homerton is heavily invested in its sport and offers a wide variety from rowing, to football and even ultimate frisbee! Each student can choose how much time they wish to invest in sport. The Boat Club (HCBC) is a big part of the College and offers an opportunity for anyone to give rowing a try. Students can ask to set up new college teams if a sport they want to do isn't already offered by the College and funding is available to set up new clubs.

Hughes Hall

Founded: 1885

Famous Alumni: Annette Brooke, Tom Ransley, Alan Leong

Undergraduates: ~150   **Postgraduates:** ~710

Accommodation: The accommodation at Hughes Hall is varied in age and location. The PGCE students (student teachers) tend to live onsite in the original building, which is very charming, but space is somewhat limited in the rooms themselves. The kitchens, however, are pretty big and contain all the modern amenities. These rooms are also conveniently located close to the library and student-run bar (more on this below).

The Fenner's building, on the other hand, was built relatively recently and is also located on the main college site. It's modern and spacious and tends to be where MBAs, post-doc medics, and undergraduates live. It's in a great location with the dining hall below and cricket pitch next door.

Over the last five years, Hughes Hall has also opened a new building on the other side of the cricket grounds, which has brand spanking new rooms and amenities. It's a short 5-minute walk from the main college site.

Bar: Also renovated within the last 10 years, Hughes Hall's bar is a favourite among students. Located in the original college building, it's small, student-run and very popular on both weekdays and weekends. The MCR (student run college committee) regularly holds themed bops (parties) here on Friday and Saturday nights. The rest of the time, you'll often find people hanging out, playing an informal foosball game and enjoying a pint with friends.

Chapel & Religion: Hughes Hall doesn't have its own chapel. Instead, students can use the one at Emmanuel College, which is about a 10-minute walk or 5-minute bike ride away. Hughes Hall does, however, have its own prayer room.

Food: The food at Hughes Hall varies in quality but tends to be good, especially at formal hall. Brunch on Saturdays and Sundays is also super popular. The kitchens are well kitted out, so if you do want to cook for yourself, you have ample opportunity to do so.

Formality: Hughes Hall is very casual and friendly! No need to stand on parade here.

Grants and Bursaries: Financial aid is available for some subjects, but these are very specific and limited in number.

Location: Hughes Hall is located away from the hustle and bustle of town, but within walking or biking distance. Its location is great if you're athletically inclined; Hughes Hall is situated right behind the sports centre and cricket pitch. It's also fantastic if you love trying new foods and supporting local businesses; Hughes Hall is just off Mill Road, which is a melting pot of cool independent shops and restaurants. Finally, if you fancy going on an adventure, the train station is close by; around a 10-minute bike ride away.

Politics & Reputation: Politics doesn't play too big a role in Hughes Hall, but if you're interested in political discussion, you're bound to find someone else willing to listen and debate with. Hughes Hall is one of several 'mature colleges', which means students are all over the age of 21. It's also well-known for its large number of sportsmen and women...

Sport: Sports are big at Hughes Hall; whether competitive or for fun. We usually have one or two men in the Cambridge boat race each year. We also have an abundance of rugby players, football players, dancers, badminton players...you name it, we play it!

Jesus College

Founded: 1496, on the site of the twelfth-century Benedictine nunnery of St Mary and St Radegund by John Alcock

Famous Alumni: Thomas Cramner, Samuel Taylor, Tobias Rustat, John Worthington Laurence Sterne, Thomas Robert, Malthus Samuel, Taylor Coleridge, Sir John Sutton, Henry Arthur Morgan, Sir Alan Cottrell, Jacob Bronowski, Lisa Jardine

Undergraduates: ~450   **Postgraduates:** ~400

Accommodation: Accommodation at Jesus is really good, College owned rooms are available all years of your study. Whilst many colleges have colonies of accommodation further afield from the central site, Jesus owns the houses on the surrounding streets, so you are always very near the heart of the college. First year accommodation is all en-suite and in the main college. In second and third year you can choose where to live, either within college again, with en-suite options, or in the houses that have more privacy. All accommodation has been recently renovated and has large well-furbished kitchens which is unusual and there are full sports fields onsite which is rare particularly for a central college.

Bar: JBar is a modern bar, often rated as the best in Cambridge with a great selection of drinks and lots of cosy sitting places, in the day it transforms into the Roost Café. Price of a Pint: £2.97

Chapel & Religion: The Chapel was completed in 1245 and is the oldest chapel in Cambridge. There are daily morning prayer services and two Sunday services followed either by free breakfast or in the evening complementary drinks. There is Choral evensong three times a week also followed by drinks. The Chaplin is heavily involved in college life both on a tutorial level and through creating a full term card of events and interesting talks. The chapel is also used for other college events such as Blues and Chill, a few times a term the very talented college cohort puts on a concert which is great to go to and simply relax on a beanbag.

College Payment System: Accommodation fees can be paid through the college website by bank transfer or alternate methods can be inquired about. In college your student card can be topped up online and used to pay for meals in the dining room, and food and drinks in the café and bar.

Food: College food is of a very high standard and served within the main formal hall so always a beautiful experience. There are multiple options at lunch and dinner everyday, including vegetarian and vegan options as well as a salad bar and cold sandwich selection. Every Saturday and Sunday college brunch replaces lunch and is absolutely delicious and great to go to with friends. The prices are low around £2-4 for a main and sides however the kitchen fixed charge is very high. During exam term there is also daily breakfast. All accommodation also has access to well equipped kitchens so you can cook for yourself.

Formality: There are many fun formal events constantly happening at College. Formals happen five times a week, a delicious 3-course meal is served followed by coffee and chocolates, you can bring you own bottle of drink and it only costs £7.80 very cheap for a formal. There are also breakfasts with the master if you are involved in some college sports occasionally, yearly subject dinners and more frequent subject drinks which are all complementary.

Grants and Bursaries: Jesus offers a variety of generous travel grants and scholarships for involvement in sports. Bursaries are also available.

Location: The college is situated fairly centrally, around a 5 minute walk from Sainsburys and the centre of town, whilst not being on the main row of colleges on Trumpington street which can be overrun by Tourists.

Politics & Reputation: Jesus is known as a big friendly college due to all the grounds as well as sporty with onsite sports facilities.

Sport: Jesus is a very sporty college, unusual in having all sports fields on site including; lacrosse pitch, 3 tennis/netball courts, a rugby pitch, football pitch and a squash court. The on-site sports fields means it is easy to participate and therefore more people do, a great atmosphere. The college gym is also very well equipped and ran with both cardio and weights room and is free of charge.

King's College

Founded: 1441

Famous Alumni: Rupert Brooke, John Maynard Keynes, Alan Turing, Zadie Smith

Undergraduates: ~400   **Postgraduates:** ~250

Accommodation: There is a range from modern rooms in hostels in the city centre, to older rooms in college. You will have a choice between en-suite or shared bathroom, or a set – a bedroom plus a dining room/sitting room. Many rooms in college boast a beautiful view across the river, while others give a view across the town. Unlike some other colleges, at King's the room ballot is not based on your grades.

Food: The food at King's is quite good. Breakfast ranges from everything from a full English to yogurt and fruit so even with allergies or dietary requirements there is definitely something available for all. For lunch there are four options of meals with a vegetarian and/or vegan meal always included and for dinner there is an option of three meals with at least one vegetarian or vegan dish.

Allergy information is always listed and we are sent a preview of the meal in advance each week. Formals once a week are a big deal at King's, particularly because the food is absolutely delicious! Additionally, students are free to join the catering committee to discuss potential changes to the menu if they so desire.

Bar: Medium costs, friendly bartenders, with a lovely range of drinks. Students will also have access to a college wine cellar.

Price of a Pint: £2.50

Chapel & Religion: A beautiful and well-known chapel, with a kind and empathetic chaplain who is a source of pastoral care irrespective of your faith. The chapel is C of E, but is open to all – there are frequent inter-faith discussion groups hosted by the chaplain, on topics from body image in religious text to punk rock.

College Payment System: Pay termly for rent, if you wish to eat in the dining hall you can scan your college card to pay for food – this is billed at the end of term.

Food: All accommodation has shared kitchens, but you will also have access to eat casually in the historic dining hall for breakfast, lunch, and dinner (if you want) – as well as formal dinners.

Formality: Informal – King's strikes a balance between retaining the tradition of a Cambridge college whilst rejecting some of the most elitist aspects of the institution.

Grants and Bursaries: Generous bursaries are available, as well as a travel grant that all undergraduates are entitled to. Additionally there are funds and prizes for research and essay writing available throughout the year.

Location: In the centre of Cambridge, near to most things.

Politics & Reputation: Very liberal reputation, we have active and vocal societies for politics, feminism, worker's rights, LGBTQ+, the environment and more! In addition there is extensive welfare provision and support in King's. Until recently, there was even a communist flag in the bar (it may yet return)!

Sport: There are many college sports teams that you can join, including (but not limited to): Football, lacrosse, hockey, canoe + kayaking, mountaineering, and rugby.

Lucy Cavendish College

Founded: 1965

Famous Alumni: Noeleen Heyzer, Rosena Allin-Khan MP

Undergraduates: ~150   **Postgraduates:** ~200

Accommodation: Accommodation is offered for all students, for every year of your degree, and there's a choice of en-suite, sets (bedrooms plus living room) shared between 2 people, houses, or flats for families and couples. Every year there's a room ballot for continuing students to choose their room, and it's not based on results but is organised into 'Tiers' depending on your year and course of study. Since we're a modern college you don't get so much of the plumbing and heating problems that come with living in old buildings!

Food: The kitchens are great – I thought all colleges had hobs, ovens and freezers but apparently it's a luxury!? (I didn't even realise this until I talked to friends from different colleges). I feel really lucky to be able to de-stress via cooking whenever I like. The food in hall is great too. They have great veggie options like Mac 'n' Cheese (with sundried tomatoes and spinach! Mmmm!), and the potatoes and soup and salad bar are awesome. The kitchen staff are also lovely!

Formality: Lucy is very casual and relaxed.

Location: Lucy Cavendish is one of the newer colleges, so it's out of the centre of town, which can be frustrating to get places, but does keep the tourist away. Being all over 21 as well, we like to think that we're mature enough to cope with a short cycle ride!

Magdalene College

Founded: 1428

Famous Alumni: Samuel Pepys, Monty Don, Stella Creasy

Undergraduates: ~340   **Postgraduates:** ~230

Accommodation: The rooms in Magdalene are a mixture of bedsits and sets (i.e. separate bedroom from living/working area) with some en-suites. The rooms are divided into price bands, from 1* to 5. The vast majority of the rooms will have a sink (unless it's an en-suite) and a mini-fridge. Some of the undergraduates live in "The Village"; a collection of buildings just across the road from the Porters' Lodge. All of Magdalene's accommodation is very close together (a maximum of three minutes walk from the main college site) which helps to create a close, community feel. Magdalene guarantees accommodation for three or four years, dependent on the course. In subsequent years, rooms are chosen by a ballot. Half way through the year, the names of students are drawn in a random order, and rooms are picked according to that order. For third year rooms, this ballot order is reversed. It is possible to ballot alone, or in a group of up to eight people.

Food: Pretty good! Every day hot and cold meals are served in Ramsay dining hall at breakfast, lunch and dinner, for very reasonable prices. There are always three or so options, which cover dietary requirements such as vegetarian or vegan, but the best thing about Ramsay is the chance to catch up with friends over a meal. This is especially true at weekends, when the very popular 'brunch' is served. Everyone also has access to small communal kitchens near their rooms, and many students enjoy cooking for themselves. Formal Hall at Magdalene is the chance to have a delicious three course meal in the candlelit 16th century hall, for only £6.50 currently! A real treat, offered every night, though people mainly go to celebrate birthdays.

Location: Minutes from the centre of town, and right by the river, with punts for free hire. One of the best in Cambridge.

Murray Edwards College

Founded: 1885

Famous Alumni: Annette Brooke, Tom Ransley, Alan Leong

Undergraduates: ~150   **Postgraduates:** ~710

Accommodation: The first years are all in the same block so it is really easy to get to know all the fellow freshers. The rooms in this block are really nice, all of them have an en-suite and my room even has a balcony! After your first year, you're put in a random room ballot which is flipped the next year so it is fair for everyone. There are a range of options available, including some college owned houses that have their own gardens.

Chapel & Religion: Murray Edwards doesn't have its own chapel. Instead, students can use the one at Churchill College, which is about a 10-minute walk or 5-minute bike ride away.

Food: At Murray Edwards you have the choice to go to fabulous looking Dome for food or cook something up in the kitchens available in accommodation - meals are paid for individually rather than in a lump sum per term, which gives you the flexibility to choose to cook as much or as little as you like. The Dome food is delicious - there is always a meat, fish and vegetarian option and there are themed days through the week: for example roast dinner on Sundays, world foods on Thursday and the university-famous College Brunch on Saturday mornings, voted Cambridge's favourite brunch in a survey by The Cambridge Student newspaper.

Formality: Very welcoming and relaxed. We're encouraged to "hop, skip, and jump" on the lawns, which is very unusual for Cambridge!

Location: Castle Hill, a five minute cycle from the town centre.

Newnham College

Founded: 1871

Famous Alumni: Dame Emma Thompson, Diane Abbott, Clare Balding, various politicians, writers, professors and actresses

Undergraduates: ~400   **Postgraduates:** ~150

Accommodation: There's a brand new accommodation block called Dorothy Garrod, which have many modern double and en-suite rooms. Accommodation overall is very highly rated at Newnham, with no ugly accommodation – whatever year you are in, you will have a room with more than enough space. They are very good at providing for disabilities and other access requirements. All students will live in college all the time, with all accommodation blocks having access to a kitchen with a hob and an oven, which is not the case at most colleges!

Bar: The bar functions as the Iris Café during the day, which is very modern and popular with all students across Cambridge. The café is run by external staff, providing snacks, pastries and hot drinks like any other café. As a student run bar, it is not as popular, unless there is an event on, which happens fairly regularly.

Price of a Pint: ~£2.20

Chapel & Religion: The college itself does not have a chapel (as women's only colleges weren't allowed their own chapels), but it shares Selwyn's chapel – and its choir. The college itself is open to all religions and is in the process of making its own prayer room too. Accommodation requirements are also very generous to people requiring their own en-suites for religious purposes, etc.

College Payment System: College bills are paid every term, including accommodation and kitchen fixed charge, like most colleges. The buttery has its own prepaid system, using your student card – the more money you prepay, the less the kitchen fixed charge is. Separate money can be added for the café.

ULTIMATE OXBRIDGE COLLEGE GUIDE — CAMBRIDGE COLLEGES

Food: Eating facilities are separate to the main formal hall, with one meat, one veggie, one vegan and one fish option daily for lunch and dinner. No breakfast is available, but the café is open. Brunch is served on the weekends, like most colleges. Quality of food varies, and costs are about average for a Cambridge college. Formal Hall is once a week, costing £12.50 for students and a bit more for guests, with food quality varying here too. Cooking facilities are pretty good wherever you are in college, so if buttery food isn't up to your taste, you can definitely get by cooking all of your meals!

Formality: Newnham is a very friendly and relaxed college, compared to most colleges. The staff are all very approachable. All grass can be walked upon, which is a rarity at Cambridge!

Grants and Bursaries: Many grants and bursaries are available for those who are eligible. The college offers many opportunity funds for travelling. The JCR offers a Clubs and Societies grant, as well as a Sports persons grant, along with a gender expression fund that's been set up this year!

Location: It is very convenient for Humanities students, as it is just across from Sidgwick Site, and is just a 10 minute walk from the town centre as well as STEM lecture sites. There is a small Co-op 5 minutes away too.

Politics & Reputation: Newnham is very liberal and open-minded in general, so everyone will feel comfortable here, no matter what political background you are from. Newnham's reputation mainly comes from being one of two all female colleges and having a very popular café as well as beautiful gardens!

Sport: Newnham's boat club is one the most highly rated boat clubs in Cambridge, as well as offering other sports, such as hockey (joint with St John's), netball, football, etc. As a big college, it is one of the few colleges with its own sports grounds on site!

Pembroke College

Founded: 1347

Famous Alumni: Ted Hughes, Tom Hiddleston, William Pitt the Younger, Jo Cox MP

Undergraduates: ~440   **Postgraduates:** ~250

Accommodation: All first year undergraduates live in College. Second and third years rooms are allocated via a ballot (in groups of up to four, reversed the following year) and many end in houses further out from college in 2nd year, followed by more central houses in 3rd year. There is a choice of older or more modern rooms, but both types are spacious, with decent rent prices, and have shared bathrooms and kitchens (gyps).

Bar: The café/bar is linked to our JP (common room), which has a friendly, relaxed feel with pool, foosball, sofas and a TV room. During the daytime, students can work in the café, and in the evenings the JP is a space for socialising and gathering pre- and post- formals. It also hosts the bi-termly bops, which are a massive hit, with most students in attendance!

Price of a Pint: £3.20

Chapel & Religion: Pembroke has a gorgeous chapel and choir, who sing two services a week, go on regular tours, produce recordings and enjoy free singing lessons and weekly formals.

College Payment System: There are termly college bills- you pay rent (9 week licence) and kitchen fixed charge in advance of the term. Hall meals are put onto your student card, and you can top this up and track your expenses via an app/website. You can go down to -£100, which eventually ends up on your next college bill.

Food: We really love our food at Pembroke. Breakfast, lunch and dinner are served every weekday in hall with 2 or 3 vegetarian/vegan options as well meat options, a pasta dish and a salad bar. Brunch and dinner are served on the weekends, and the former has a reputation of being the best in Cambridge, although all Pembroke students will tell you that breakfast is actually better, with custom-made pancakes, omelettes and paninis! Don't let the nickname of our servery, 'trough', deceive you- the food is wonderful, which makes up for the lack of ovens in gyps. Formals are £10 for students and truly delicious. Other stand out food-related events include subject dinners, boat club dinners, and Tutor Tea (a termly opportunity to talk pastoral care and enjoy free afternoon tea)!

Formality: Pembroke holds Formal Hall every evening, and it has a fairly sophisticated atmosphere, including gowns. Alternating May Balls and June Events are lavish end of term celebrations, and Pembroke has a reputation for hosting amazing balls at a reasonable price. Overall, the students and staff are still very relaxed and friendly, whilst enjoying formal Oxbridge traditions.

Grants and Bursaries: Pembroke offers a very generous range of grants and financial awards to eligible students, including materials grants, travel grants, sports awards, equipment expenses, and hardships grants and loans. There are also opportunities for paid employment.

Location: Very central- between Downing and New Museums site so very convenient for science students- a 30 second hop to lectures from bed! Around a 5 minute cycle to Sidgwick site and the UL. Everywhere is very manageable by foot from Pembroke – including the station, and importantly, the clubs!

Politics & Reputation: There are people from all backgrounds who hold a wide range of political views, but the atmosphere is very open and non-judgemental, so you get to experience lots of interesting discussions. Our reputation revolves around good food, beautiful buildings, a convenient location and friendly people.

Sport: Pembroke has many sports clubs, from Netball to Hockey to Squash, with practices usually taking place in the Pembroke sports grounds a short cycle away. Both men's and women's football have been particularly successful in intercollege leagues in recent years. There is also a gym in College, and opportunities for leisurely sports such as Yoga and Zumba. Pembroke College Boat Club is also very successful and has held many headships in May Bumps, yet is very welcoming to all students and always proves popular with novice freshers!

Peterhouse

Founded: 1284 (oldest Cambridge college!)

Famous Alumni: Lord Kelvin; Henry Cavendish; Thomas Campion; Thomas Gray; Sam Mendes; David Mitchell; Colin Greenwood (amongst others)

Undergraduates: ~200   **Postgraduates:** ~116

Accommodation: Peterhouse has amazing accommodation. Practically all of it is on-site and all freshers are housed together in either St Peter's Terrace (SPT) or the William Stone Building (WSB) just a 4 minute walk away from the main college site, creating a really close-knit community. En-suites are available for all three years. Fresher accommodation is randomly allocated, however in the following years students participate in a room ballot. Points are allocated for both academic grades and extra-curriculars – this determines the placing in the ballot. Kitchen facilities are limited in first year (kettle, toaster, microwave) although hobs are available in 2nd/3rd/4th year accommodation.

Bar: The college bar opens at 7pm every day and is a very popular place to go to after Formal Hall or before nights out. It is located next to the JCR in the Whittle Building and therefore is usually bustling with people. Price of a Pint: £2.90

Chapel & Religion: The Peterhouse Chapel is a beautiful candlelit 17th century building and serves as the focus for a welcoming community, open for people from all denominations and none. The Chapel plays an active role in student life with weekly breakfasts, bible studies and various Chapel Suppers, as well as the yearly Chapel retreat. The Chapel Choir is friendly and receives regular visitors due to its very high-quality music.

College Payment System: College bills are paid via a bank transfer. Food and drink is bought through your student card, which at the beginning of term is automatically topped up with a minimum spend requirement of around £100.

Food: All meals are provided in the beautiful 13th century hall and tend to cost around £2-4, and there are always vegetarian/vegan options. Formal Hall occurs daily in Full Term and costs around £6.70 for members of the college. For special occasions the Catering department organises Super-halls, which are very fancy five-course meals.

Formality: Peterhouse has a small but very close community and although the college is the oldest and therefore has a deep sense of tradition the atmosphere amongst students is very relaxed and friendly. In particular the Deer Park in college provides a large green space for students to walk through, which is an appreciated contrast to the more formal courts.

Grants and Bursaries: Peterhouse is incredibly wealthy relative to its small size and students are therefore extremely lucky to be able to apply for or request a variety of loans and grants for reasons including hardship, language learning and travel.

Location: Peterhouse is in an ideal location: in town, however far enough away that we are not swarmed with tourists! There's a corner shop right opposite the college, but otherwise Sainsbury's is about a 10-15 minute walk away.

Politics & Reputation: Peterhouse used to have a reputation for being slightly conservative and traditional, however this is not reflective of the college nowadays in the slightest. The diverse student body comprises people with various backgrounds and interests, which allows for really interesting discussions.

Sport: Sport at Peterhouse is relatively low-key due to its small size, so the environment is perfect for anyone wanting to get involved with sport in a more relaxed way. Most teams don't require training during the week – the real involvement occurs on the weekends when the matches take place. Nevertheless, the college has some fantastic athletes and our Boat Club in particular performs exceptionally well!

Queens' College

Founded: 1448

Famous Alumni: Stephen Fry, Erasmus, Emily Maitlis

Undergraduates: ~500   **Postgraduates:** ~500

Accommodation: A major plus to Queens' is that you are guaranteed good accommodation on college site for all three years if you want it! The vast majority of freshers chose to all live in Cripps court with a choice between en-suite or your own bathroom but across the hall (cheaper). This large building means you can 'gyp-hop' walking through connecting kitchens and visit anyone in your year without leaving the building! Whilst Cripps rooms are not the biggest compared to some in other colleges this is more than made up for the huge social benefits and proximity to buttery the first year accommodation brings.

Rooms for second and third year are based on a random ballot. Most second years chose to go for a 'shared set' in second year which are all in one building. This means that the strong social aspect to Queens' accommodation continues into second year! The third year rooms are not all in one building, rather a few building across the river are designated for third years. Note that these are some of the best in college, in your third year you could find yourself with a shared living room! Bar: The bar functions as the Iris Café during the day, which is very modern and popular with all students across Cambridge. The café is run by external staff, providing snacks, pastries and hot drinks like any other café. As a student run bar it is not as popular, unless there is an event on, which happens fairly regularly.

Food: Queens' offers facilities for students to be self-catered or catered as they choose. In all three years small kitchens are located on each landing with basic cooking facilities; including a hob, microwave, toaster and fridges, although admittedly there are no ovens or freezers which can make cooking larger meals difficult. Nonetheless, the college dining hall (often referred to as buttery), provides breakfast, lunch and dinner and is generally high quality. The price of an evening meal currently averages at around £3.50, and the famous Queens' brunch on the weekend is a particular highlight, with 8 items for just £2.50, everyone loves brunch! Formal hall is a special addition to college dining, this is a served, three-course meal which students attend to celebrate events such as birthdays, and currently costs £9. It's also pretty exciting as you get to wear your gown and feel as though you're in Harry Potter. In all aspects of catering the college is attentive to dietary requirements, and provides options for vegetarians and kosher/halal etc.

Formality: The thing that struck me when I first came to Queens' is just how laid-back and welcoming everyone is here. When you arrive in Freshers' Week, you'll be given college "parents", two second-year students who will help you and about four other freshers, your "siblings", find your way around. You'll do lots of things together as a college family in the first few days, like punting, afternoon tea and a tour of Cambridge full of useful tips, and having some friendly faces there right from the start makes it so much more enjoyable.

You have the freedom and support to pursue any of your interests, no matter how quirky, and I've met some fascinating people. It may be one of the oldest colleges, but Queens' is far from stuffy or traditional.!

Location: Siting on both sides of the river, Queens' is one of the .most central and prettiest colleges. It is also features the mathematical bridge, which according to legend was built by Newton, without any nails, and is held together by maths alone!

Sport: Most popular sports and clubs are organised on an inter-college basis so there is at least one competitive team at Queens' for rugby, football, rowing, netball, hockey, lacrosse, tennis etc. Sport is also played at a more informal, less competitive level, where everyone enjoys participating. Queens' also have their own squash courts available for use at any time.

Robinson College

Founded: 1977

Famous Alumni: Nick Clegg (politician), Robert Webb (comedian, actor), Konnie Huq (Blue Peter presenter) – we are a fairly new college!

Undergraduates: ~400   **Postgraduates:** ~160

Accommodation: There are four tiers of room-value, (£1380 per term) standard (£1680), standard plus (£1845, with an en-suite), best (£2075, large with an en-suite). Although a little pricier than other colleges, there are no fixed kitchen fees nor charges for utilities. Accommodation is one of Robinson's strongest points as the rooms for each tier are mostly the same style with the same amenities, unlike other colleges where you pay the same price for drastically different rooms. There are also enough rooms for you to stay on site for all three or four years of your degree. In comparison, some other colleges only have enough rooms centrally for the first year, such that in other years you are spread out around Cambridge in houses owned by the colleges, and these can be up to a 20-minute walk away from the central site.

At Robinson all rooms are also close to each other, so you are never more than a 5-minute walk away from your friends. For people in second year and above, you can opt to live in houses owned by Robinson at the back of the college, a 5-minute walk away, which are less campus-like and more homely. Finally, rooms are allocated through a randomly allocated system where you can ballot with friends, unlike some other colleges that allocate based on academic performance. Each room shares a kitchen with 4 or 5 people that are fully equipped, although most do not have ovens.

Bar: The bar is called the 'Red Brick Café Bar'. Hot bar food is served every day, with paninis, pizzas, sandwiches and snacks on the roll. They also sell common amenities such as toothpaste. A great range of hot drinks are also available. Alcoholic drinks are available until late in the bar. The bar also has a pool table and regular quizzes and karaoke are held here, run by the bar manager.

Price of a Pint: ~£1.90, one of the cheapest college bars in Cambridge.

Chapel & Religion: There is a modern chapel with a beautiful stain glass window. The Chapel also houses a world renowned Frobenius organ, a harpsichord by David Rubio and a Steinway piano. There is a flourishing orchestra and music society that make good use of this stunning chapel.

College Payment System: EPOS (electronic point of sale) – with your university card.

Food: The catering facilities are another of Robinson's strongest points. There is amazing food, in price, range, taste, and quantity. Vegetarian and vegan options are always available. It is reasonably priced and as there is no fixed kitchen charge you can choose to come and go as you please. Brunch is also served every Saturday and Sunday, but unlike most other colleges, lunch is also served alongside the English fry-up. We also have bi-weekly formals that are slightly more expensive than some other colleges but serve a spectacular three course meal. The setting may have less grandeur, but it is well worth it for the food. The portions, as always, are very hearty. Plus, there are no corkage fees, which many colleges enforce.

Formality: Robinson is an incredibly friendly and relaxed college, with the staff and students helping to create this warm atmosphere. The staff are very receptive to student input thus we have one of the most active JCRs in Cambridge. Robinson also maintains a beautiful garden and all grass can be walked upon. There is also a croquet lawn open in the summer.

Grants and Bursaries: There are some fantastic grants available, such as for summer research and sport, and prizes for succeeding in academics in addition to bursaries for those that financially qualify. However, Robinson is one of the newest colleges so does not have innumerable wealth such as Trinity, so the range of funds is more limited.

Location: Robinson is slightly outside of town, being only a 10-minute walk or 5-minute cycle into the centre. It is however right next door to the university library, sports centre, and humanities lecture site (Sidgwick Site). Is also well placed to access the mathematics department and veterinary department. The location also means it is luckily not disturbed by tourists.

Politics & Reputation: Robinson is one of the most open-minded and liberal colleges. It is best known for having good food, a tight knit community, being incredibly homely and LGBTQ+ friendly. Our nickname is the 'red brick college' because we do indeed have many red bricks, which to some adds to the warm nature.

Sport: We have a college club for most sports, including netball, hockey, lacrosse, rowing, ultimate frisbee, tennis, badminton, croquet, rugby, and football. We are also right next to the University Sports Centre, and have our own netball pitches a 10-minute cycle away.

Selwyn College

Founded: 1882

Famous Alumni: Hugh Laurie, Robert Harris, Wes Streeting

Undergraduates: ~380   **Postgraduates:** ~260

Accommodation: All first-year rooms are en-suite. About half of other rooms are en-suite. There is a wide range of rental brackets based on the size of your room, but all the rooms are of a high quality and are well-maintained.

Bar: gorgeous, recently renovated bar with a wide range of both standard and premium drinks Price of a Pint: £3.50

Chapel & Religion: Beautiful chapel, Anglican.

College Payment System: Pay-as-you-go food and drink in the cafeteria.

Food: Food is good and largely affordable.

Formality: Relaxed – some traditions are upheld (e.g. wearing gowns to formal events), but in general not at all stuffy (e.g. can walk on most lawns).

Grants and Bursaries: Wide variety of grants and bursaries available.

Location: Edge of town centre. 1 min away from Sidgwick site (location of most humanities faculties), 2 min away from University Library, short walk or cycle to most other faculties.

Politics & Reputation: Politics: liberal and left-wing slant, reputation: very friendly and welcoming.

Sport: Active rowing club, active rugby club (located next to the University's rugby stadium).

Sidney Sussex College

Founded: 1596

Famous Alumni: Oliver Cromwell (English civil war), Carol Vorderman (TV), Andrew Smyth (GBBO 2016) and suggested to be the fictional college of Sherlock Holmes

Undergraduates: ~350 (total)   **Postgraduates:** ~200 (total)

Accommodation: College-owned accommodation provided for all undergraduates throughout their undergraduate degrees. Vast majority of accommodation is on the central college site with a small block of freshers' accommodation 2 minutes down the road and a couple of houses/hostels that you can choose to live in during 2nd/3rd year if you wish. Essentially at Sidney if you want to live in the centre of town, you'll be able to the entire time. As all of the accommodation is on site, you'll be able to keep using college hall (for food), gym and bar throughout your degree. The rent at Sidney is amongst the cheapest with the average room at about £130 a week (going up with inflation). Most second years get en-suite rooms and third years can choose en-suite rooms too. In first year, your room is randomly allocated with other first years, in second and third year you choose it based on a randomly generated choosing order (no academic ballot – where your room depends on your grades).

Bar: The place most students, most evenings, will come to relax and socialise, whether they drink or not. Being one of the few fully student-run bars in Cambridge, it is also one of the cheapest, as well as having one of the most friendly and casual atmospheres. Pool, darts, foosball, sofas and a cosy feel make this very popular across all Cambridge students.

Price of a Pint: £2.50

Chapel & Religion: Sidney has its own very nice chapel and choir, who go on regular fully funded tours (the choir has many benefits, as well as free formals regularly). Sidney also has its own prayer room and is well known for being very open to all faiths.

College Payment System: Pay contactless with student ID card (which gets put on to your termly college bill, which you pay at the end of term) for food in hall and printing. Bar accepts cash or card.

Food: There are three meals a day during the week, brunch and dinner on Saturdays and just dinner on Sundays. Food is generally good with lots of options available and on the affordable side. A full meal in Hall costs about £4 and you can get a 4-item brunch for less than £2.50. There are also formals in Hall 3 times a week, currently priced at £9 for Sidney Students where you get a three-course meal served to you. These are fantastic value and a great way to celebrate a birthday (and cheaper than a restaurant!).

Formality: Not super formal, you cannot walk on the grass on the front courts but there are huge gardens at the back of college. Gowns are worn to Formals.

Grants and Bursaries: Lots of travel grants available. Some funding for sports. An additional bursary on top of the Cambridge Bursary Scheme for some students which grants £1000 off accommodation. Some additional automatic rent rebate for Cambridge Bursary Scheme students. As the bar is student run you can work behind the bar for extra money (which pays the living wage).

Location: Very central, opposite Sainsbury's (is extremely useful for food shopping), also close to clubs, which is nice on nights out, but not so nice if you have a room facing the main street due to noise from street performers in the day and clubs at night. Closer to classes for Science and Maths students, but not far (maximum 15 minute walk almost anywhere!) for other subjects. Even without a bicycle, you will be well placed.

Politics & Reputation: Politics is not a major talking point at Sidney due to the friendly and non-judgemental atmosphere. You will meet people from all backgrounds and areas, with no judgements as to whether you are Northern/Southern/International, Tory/Labour/etc, etc. Sidney is one of the few colleges where you can almost ensure you will meet a group of people you will get along with, and a group of friends for life, with such a varied cohort!

Sport: Sidney tend to have joint college teams with other colleges, due to its small size, but this is a positive for meeting new like-minded people! All sports are played at college and you are almost guaranteed to meet at least a couple people playing the sport you are interested in at university level at Sidney!

As mentioned before, lots of financial and moral support is given to people playing sports (as well as doing choir, music or drama!

St Catherine's College

Founded: 1473

Famous Alumni: Jeremy Paxman, Richard Ayoade, Ian McKellen

Undergraduates: ~400   **Postgraduates:** ~150

Accommodation: First and third years at Catz live in college, and have a choice of either en-suite or non en-suite rooms of varying sizes. Before first years arrive, they are given a choice of an en-suite room, or a small, medium or large non en-suite room. Students living in non en-suite rooms will usually share a bathroom with around 6-8 people, but all rooms have a sink. En-suite and non en-suite alike, you can still personalise and decorate your room with photo collages, posters, cushions and make it feel like home! Second years at Catz live with their friends in flats of 4 or 5 on a separate site- St Chad's, a 10 minute walk from college

Food: All three meals can be purchased daily. Meals are hearty, with meat-and-two-veg being common, but also a wide range of fish and vegetable dishes. There is always at least one vegetarian option, often two, and also cold food and snacks for sale. On a Sunday, brunch takes the place of breakfast and lunch; this is the best-loved meal of the week and unbelievable value.

Three times a week there's 'formal hall'. You dress up and wear your gown and eat a four-course formal meal: Catz is unique in having a cheese course.

Formality: Relaxed – some traditions are upheld (e.g. wearing gowns to formal events), but in general not at all stuffy (e.g. can walk on most lawns).

Location: Right in the centre of town, opposite Corpus. Catz is one of the smallest colleges though, so it can feel a little cramped.

St Edmund's College

Founded: 1896

Famous Alumni: Hugh Laurie, Robert Harris, Wes Streeting

Undergraduates: ~100   **Postgraduates:** ~450

Accommodation: Impressive en-suite accommodation has recently been built, and a building with rooms for couples opened in the last few years. This goes a long way towards meeting the needs of the student population, but you may still be required to live out during the intermediate years of an undergraduate degree. Those who do, either rent privately or find surplus rooms at nearby Colleges.

Formality: The academic and social environment is unpretentious. Fellows, undergrads and postgrads socialise in a single combination room and eat together. The smaller size of the college means people quickly get to know each other and there is a close-knit atmosphere at socials

Location: Lucy Cavendish is one of the newer colleges, so it's out of the centre of town, which can be frustrating to get places, but does keep the tourist away. Being all over 21 as well, we like to think that we're mature enough to cope with a short cycle ride!

Sport: Sport at College level has in recent years been marked by impressive initiative and determination from students, resulting in the college being put firmly on the map. St Edmund's boasts neither the history nor facilities of some of the older Colleges as far as rowing is concerned, yet this year the boat club won the Mitchell Cup for the most successful performance in the May Bumps races, the culmination of the college rowing calendar.

St John's College

Founded: 1511

Famous Alumni: William Wilberforce, William Wordsworth, Sir John Cockcroft, Paul Dirac, Manmohan Singh

Undergraduates: ~640   **Postgraduates:** ~220

Accommodation: The college provides accommodation both in and out of college for all its students. Room price varies from approx. £1400-£2000 per term but most rooms are at the lower end of the spectrum.

Bar: A very sociable place! It is open every day until 11pm except Fridays and Saturdays (12pm) Price of a Pint: £2-£3

Chapel & Religion: Anglican Church but not compulsory and open to all faiths.

College Payment System: Termly Invoice/Bank Transfer

Food: Three meals per day served in the Buttery everyday (£3-£5 for a meal). Formal Dinner option served in Hall daily except Saturday (£10-£13 for a three-course meal with wine). The quality of the food is very good and both the buttery and hall are very sociable areas of the college.

Formality: Gowns and smart dress required for specific events and formal hall, but otherwise no formalities.

Grants and Bursaries: St John's is one of the most generous colleges when it comes to grants and bursaries, and the college website has great information on them.

Location: Central Cambridge (almost) everything is within walking distance including faculties, shops, restaurants, clubs… John's location is a great asset.

Politics & Reputation: The reputation of being uptight and conservative does not accurately represent the college. The student body is not obviously political, and the JCR is politically diverse with a wide range of different opinions.

Sport: St John's is by far one of the best colleges when it comes to sports not only because of the amount of sports offered but also because of the high standards at which first teams play. Most popular sports include: Rowing (Lady Margaret Boat Club)-The best college boat club in Cambridge and the oldest one across the university. Rugby-Commonly known as the Redboys, John's rugby team is one of the best ones in Cambridge having won Cuppers repeatedly over the years. Football- Three teams to cater for different needs; First XI plays in first division. An overall very fun and sociable team. Other sports include: Cricket, Hockey, Lacrosse, Tennis, Netball, Athletics, Basketball, Cheerleading.

Trinity College

Founded: 1546

Famous Alumni: Niels Bohr, Bertrand Ru

Undergraduates: ~500   **Postgraduates:** ~350

Accommodation: Though it varies a lot, from having en-suites and well-equipped kitchens (ovens, hobs, microwaves etc.) to shared bathrooms and fewer cooking appliances, the rooms are all generally large and all very comfortable. Though freshers are randomly allocated a room, in second and third year students are invited to choose their room via a ballot system. In second year the ballot is random: those at the top of the list get first choice etc. The balloting system therefore allows students to pick a location they like, with their chosen appendages (en-suite/kitchen etc) and within their price range. (But don't worry, even if right at the bottom of the ballot you are guaranteed a nice room!) In third year, the second year ballot switches (if you were at the bottom you are nearer to top etc, so everyone has a chance to get their dream room.) This is complicated by the scholars (those who got firsts in their exams) ballot, as they get first choice, but after that ballot has closed the normal ballot ensues. Most Trinity students opt to live in college. Some rooms are sets, which means you get a living room as well as a bedroom, and double sets mean living with a friend and sharing a living room!

Bar: gorgeous, recently renovated bar with a wide range of both standard and premium drinks

Food: Normal hall is usually pretty good, there are three hot options a day (inc vegetarian) plus a dairy-free or gluten-free alternative. Brunch on Sundays is a major highlight of the week - especially when they do waffles. Formal hall (3x a week) is a bit hit and miss in terms of the food, but the atmosphere makes it pretty special.

Formality: Trinity can seem quite intimidating at first. One of the older colleges, its architecture and sheer size can initially overwhelm, being as beautiful as it is! But this is quickly overwritten by the friendly people who make up the college—the porters are always happy to help and the students themselves induce a homely and welcoming atmosphere.

Grants and Bursaries: Trinity is one of the wealthiest colleges, so there's a wide range available for various needs and projects.

Location: Right in the centre of town, one of the biggest colleges, and the largest undergrad populations.

Trinity Hall

Founded: 1350

Famous Alumni: Hugh Laurie, Robert Harris, Wes Streeting

Undergraduates: ~400   **Postgraduates:** ~200

Accommodation: All first-year students are guaranteed a room in the college's central site, amongst beautiful historic buildings and gardens, right in the centre of the city. This is where the library, dining hall, bar and chapel are located, along with facilities like the music room. The rooms here currently cost between £70 and £140 a week - they vary in quality, but most of them are quite nice! In subsequent years, most people have more modern rooms further out of the centre (though none of them are more than 10 minutes' bike ride away). These vary from smaller rooms with kitchens/bathrooms shared between 10ish people (around £100 a week) to large, modern rooms with en-suites (up to £145 a week). You choose your room via a randomised "ballot" system.

Food: In first year, students live on-site and have access to a small kitchen, which includes a sink, microwave, fridge and kettle. You can cook food in this kitchen, but for a proper meal students usually go to the college canteen which is also on-site and serves breakfast, lunch and dinner at certain hours (and brunch on Sundays!). The food there is good (if slightly repetitive) and not too pricey - and vegetarian, vegan, and gluten-free options are available. In second and third year accommodation, kitchens are bigger and better equipped with hobs, allowing students to cook for themselves if they want to- although students of all years are always welcome to eat in the canteen!

Location: Right next to the larger Trinity College, which makes it easy to find, .but doesn't help with people confusing the two!

Wolfson College

Founded: 1965

Famous Alumni: Eric Monkman of University Challenge fame, and many heads of state and politicians including Letsie III of Lesotho, Carrie Lam, Susan Kiefel, Song Sang-Hyun, Rupiah Banda.

Undergraduates: ~180 (all aged 21 or over)   **Postgraduates:** ~514

Accommodation: Modern en-suite rooms, all on-site at the College Campus. Lease can run either year-round, or just for term times.

Bar: Recently refurbished, centre of college social life. Price of a Pint: £3~

Chapel & Religion: None

College Payment System: Fees payable by cheque, credit card and bank transfer. Day-to-day payments at bar and dining hall by topping up student card.

Food: Highly rated among Cambridge serveries. Caters to most dietary requirements (veggie/vegan, halal, lactose intolerance, gluten free, etc.). Operates 3 meals a day, 7 days a week, both in and out of term time.

Formality: As formal as one wants it to be, it is one of the most casual of Cambridge colleges.

Grants and Bursaries: Disadvantaged student bursaries, travel grants, long-vacation project funding, and more. Many topical scholarships opportunities.

Location: Just outside the city centre, next to the Arts and Humanities departments. Situated in the fashionable neighbourhood of Newnham, and a short walk to the picturesque village of Grantchester.

Politics & Reputation: Once of the Cambridge mature colleges, admitting applicants over 21 only. Renowned as the most diverse, international, and cosmopolitan Cambridge college. The Wolfson Howlers, stand-up shows by professional comedians, are an attraction to students and residents from across the city. The College gardens are famous for their exotic plants from across the globe.

Sport: Many sports and societies: Football, rugby, squash, pole and aerobics, rock climbing, yoga and meditation, dancing (salsa, ballroom, tango, Brazilian), board games, public speaking, student gardening, LGBT and BAME societies.

OXFORD COLLEGES

There are 39 different colleges at Oxford, which we've arranged in alphabetical order across the following pages.

We've left out a couple of the PPHs, which are explained after the college profiles, and we've also not been able to give us much detail about Parks College as it's a brand-new college and doesn't have any students yet!

All of the information here was contributed by current and recent students of these colleges, so it should be all be up to date, with the possible exception of the bar prices! You'll be able to find great detail on all the colleges on their respective websites, in particular the student union sites. Most Oxford colleges has two students' unions, known as common rooms – there is normally a literal common room, hence the name – one for undergraduate, and one for graduate students. They should both have their own websites, which will provide far more detail than we were able to here.

Our goal was to provide all this information in one place, easily arranged for you to flick through and see which colleges you're interested in learning more about. We'd like to thank all of the following students who helped with these profiles, which were by far the hardest part of the book to write, so thank you to:

Aditi Shingrapure	Lucy Enderby
Alice Bennett	Lucy Wright
Amy Dunning	Magnus Fugger
Clare Tierney	Olivia Campbell
Emily Eraneva-Dibb	Rhiannon Davies
Henry Straughan	Ria Sangal
Imogen Edwards-Lawrence	Toby Bowman
Kate Coomby	Tsvetana Myagkova
Lewis Webb	Zainab Mahmood

Balliol College

Founded: 1263

Famous Alumni: Four prime ministers, including Boris Johnson, as well Richard Dawkins, and a host of Nobel laureates.

Undergraduates: ~350   **Postgraduates:** ~350

Accommodation: The college guarantees accommodation for your first and final years, and most have the option of living in college owned property in their second year. First year rooms are randomly allocated based on price band, which you choose from before you arrive. Like most other colleges, there's a random ballot for rooms in third year. If you need a carer, or a disabled access room, the college has plenty of these to make sure that everyone's needs are met.

Bar: The Lindsay Bar is the only fully student run bar left in Oxford (apart from Wolfson, but that's grad only), and all the profits are reinvested in keeping prices low. The bar is open until 11pm on weekdays, and later at weekends, and shots are only 75p on Tuesday nights! The bar also offers darts, table football, and a pool table.

Price of a Pint: £1.70

Food: Hall offer lunch and dinner everyday, and there's even cheaper food available three meals a day in the student run pantry in the JCR. All rooms are close to a kitchen or kitchenette, so you'll be able to do your own cooking easily as well.

Location: Right in the centre of town on Broad Street.

Politics & Reputation: Balliol has a long history in politics, with five prime ministers and lots of political journalists as recent alumni. Nevertheless the college is very politically open and welcoming, and much more relaxed than the 800 year old pedigree might suggest!

Sport: Balliol has a good record in sports over the past few years, with two promotions for the football team. The college offers financial support to any Blues level athletes, and the Jowett Walk annexe is one of the closest sports grounds to the city centre of any college. Student also all have access to the Iffley site, where you'll find the track where Roger Bannister ran the first four minute mile!

Brasenose College

Founded: 1509

Famous Alumni: David Cameron, Malcolm Turnbull, Michael Palin, Jessie Burton, Duncan Campbell, J. Michael Kosterlitz, Elias Ashmole (of the Ashmolean museum)

Undergraduates: ~356   **Postgraduates:** ~204

Accommodation: If you are an undergrad at Brasenose you get accommodation with the college, which can be a huge weight off your mind. In your second year you'll be housed in one of our annexes, which are a few minutes' walk from the college (you'll also be there in your fourth year, if you have one!) Most of the annexes have en-suite rooms, but not all, and the kitchens are decent. If you're a grad student, you'll be in an annexe regardless (these include rooms and flats for couples). In your first and third year, you'll be on the main site. Accommodation on the main site is more communal, with shared food storage in the hallways (rather than kitchens) and shared bathrooms. The rooms vary in quality, but there is a ballot based on randomised names, so you have a fairly good chance of getting a great room at least one year! All the accommodation includes accessible rooms for those who need them.

Bar: The College Bar

Price of a Pint: £3

Chapel & Religion: The chapel has a large and incredibly talented choir, which forms the centre of much of Chapel life at Brasenose. There are services on Sundays which everyone is welcome to attend (but not mandatory). Religion at the college can generally play as large or small a part as you would like!

College Payment System: Accommodation fees, Tuition Fees, and other things like laundry and food costs (batels) are paid termly, you can also manage your payments using the online Upay service.

Food: Students at Brasenose (Brasenostrils) love their food, there are informal meals every day, and formal ones three times a week. The food is of a really high quality, and it is affordable (a three course meal is a fiver).

Formality: The college is less formal than some, while retaining a lot of the 'wow' factor that old Oxford colleges have. Formal meals are a regular occurrence, but aren't compulsory.

Grants and Bursaries: There are substantial measures in place to support students in financial hardship at Brasenose, including subsidies for living costs, travel, resources, and bursaries. There is also a fund for students who wish to stay in college during the vacation.

Location: Brasenose is in the best location in Oxford, about 10 metres from the Radcliffe Camera at the heart of the university. It is also right next to the Exam Schools and a lot of great bars, restaurants, and pubs.

Politics & Reputation: Brasenose is increasingly diverse, and there is ripe ground for political debate regardless of where you are on the spectrum, though it tends towards the conservative. The atmosphere is one of intellectual pursuit, so people try to be open minded, and are open to discussion! The reputation (besides the lucky college in the best spot in town) is that we are a nice bunch! Brasenose came first in the Oxford Barometer survey for friendliness, we also have stunning architecture and great food!

Sport: Sport at Brasenose is available for everyone regardless of ability, or the level of commitment you want to invest. We have teams and sports clubs for a wide variety of sports, and access to the university gym is included free of charge.

Christ Church

Founded: 1546

Famous Alumni: 13 Prime Ministers (Peel + Gladstone), 10 chancellors of the exchequer, King Edward VII, 17 archbishops, John Locke, Albert Einstein, Sir William Osler ('father of modern medicine'), Jacob Rothschild, David Dimbleby, Lewis Carroll, Riz Ahmed (actor) – take your pick!

Undergraduates: ~442   **Postgraduates:** ~203

Accommodation: You can spend all three years in college accommodation, though for most people 1 or 2 of those years will be in the college annexes (one across the road, and one by Iffley sports ground). Rooms are allocated by random ballot, with scholars and musicians getting first pick. The fee for all rooms are the same. If you are high on the ballot, you may get to choose a 'pec set'. These are shared rooms with a large living room area. You are only allowed to live in a pec set for one year.

Bar: The atmosphere for the bar can be quite hit and miss. Typically, the bar reps are very dedicated and arrange lots of events which are very good fun, but on off nights the bar can be quite empty.

Price of a Pint: £2

Chapel & Religion: The only college with a cathedral inside it, as a student you can go to evensongs and special services that could otherwise be quite exclusive. The Dean is the head of the college and the cathedral. If you go to evensong you get free wine at dinner afterwards!!

College Payment System: Breakfast and Lunch is paid by item, dinner you either opt in or opt out of. If you opt in, you pay for every meal, even ones you don't manage to attend, if you opt out you only pay for the dinners that you go to but they are more expensive. If you opt in the three course meals will cost you about £3!! There is also a tab system for the Buttery (the bar) which gets added onto your termly batels

Food: The food is pretty good. Brunch is quite the event on weekends as you can get a lot of food for not much money. Otherwise the dinners are generally pretty good. There's also a café in the JCR which does fantastic paninis

Formality: Christ Church is one of the most formal colleges. Formal hall works a bit differently to other colleges as there is one every night and the food is the same as informal. What is different is Guest Dinner, which happens twice a term, is black tie and has a fantastic four course menu

Grants and Bursaries: Christ Church is very good at supporting its students financially, with a generous hardship fund, free money for books, travel grants, sports grants – there's a lot to support whatever it is you are doing.

Location: Right in the centre of town on St Aldates

Politics & Reputation: Christ Church is seen as one of the poshest colleges and people you meet from other colleges will likely have negative prejudices against you because of that reputation. Usually after 5 minutes they'll realise that it is more fiction than fact!

Sport: Christ Church has fantastic resources for sports. You can reserve punts, tennis courts, squash courts, and a multipurpose astro-turf pretty much whenever you like for free. Christ Church's facilities are also some of the most central of all the colleges – even more central than the university's own centralised facilities! The meadows are also yours to use freely so you can use them for a kick about or whatever without having to make a reservation and it's on your doorstep.

Corpus Christi College

Founded: 1517

Famous Alumni: Isiah Berlin, Thomas Nagel, and both Miliband brothers!

Undergraduates: ~250   **Postgraduates:** ~90

Accommodation: Corpus offers college accommodation for all three years of your degree, which is more generous than most other colleges.

Bar: The Corpus Beer Cellar, known as the BC, which has student bar staff as well as Lance, the resident barman. We have darts and pool, and some of the most reasonably priced drinks in Oxford!

Price of a Pint: £2

Food: The hall serves three meals a day, which you pay for by topping up your Bod card. Lunch is £2.49, and dinner only £3.09. Dinner is replaced with formal hall on Fridays, although you'll need to enter the ballot for a place. You'll get priority if you're welcoming guests though.

Formality: Corpus is one of the smallest colleges at Oxford, which gives it a friendly, intimate atmosphere. You'll end up knowing everyone pretty quickly, grad students included, which you won't get at one of the bigger colleges.

Grants and Bursaries: Corpus has a range of grants and bursaries, including a £150pa Academic Expenses Grant for books, equipment and application fees, a travel grant of £450 each student (£600 for 4 year degrees), and awards 3 scholarships to 'expand students horizons' of £5,000 each year.

Location: Just behind the more famous Christ Church, between Merton fields and Merton Street.

Exeter College

Founded: 1314

Famous Alumni: J. R. R. Tolkien, Sir Philip Pullman, Reeta Chakrabarti, Sir Roger Bannister, Richard Burton, Sydney Brenner, Ronald Cohen

Undergraduates: ~357   **Postgraduates:** ~262

Accommodation: 1st Year: On the main site for all freshers, 2nd Year: 40% of the year stay in college owned Student Houses of 8-9 people. These houses are about a 20-minute walk away from the main college site, but as most people cycle, it's much quicker. Depending on their position in the Housing Ballot, the rest of the year can either choose to stay on the main college site or move to Cohen Quad in Jericho (a modern facility with all en-suite bathrooms and a shared kitchen for each floor). In either students' 3rd or 4th years they are given priority in the Housing Ballot with most choosing to stay in Cohen Quad and some back on the main college site. College provided accommodation is guaranteed for 3 years.

Bar: Quite a cosy and a very social place! Breakfast and Lunch are available here for reasonable prices cheaper than the dining Hall. The customisable panini bar is a big hit, as well as game of pool or darts for a study break. The bar is the centre of social events in college, hosting regular open mic nights, karaoke, bops as well as football, rugby and charity drinks-which all have great atmospheres.

Price of a Pint: ~ £2.30

Chapel & Religion: One of the most beautiful Chapels in Oxford (featured in the film Dr. Strange!) and is a space for both those who are religious and non-religious. Our Chaplain is very approachable; in terms of discussing both religious and non-religious topics; from sending us podcasts and music for meditation to hosting Pancake day on Shrove Tuesday. There are weekly choral Evensong services sung by the choir and at Christmas the Carol Service is not to be missed.

College Payment System: Accommodation bills are paid at the beginning of every term. Throughout term, food from the bar, Hall or café in Cohen Quad are paid for using our University ID card which can be topped-up online. However, laundry machines on both the main site and Cohen Quad require exact change.

Food: On the main site, both hot and cold breakfast and lunch are available in the bar. During the week, lunch and dinner are also available in the dining hall and usually there are 3 main options (2 meat and 1 vegetarian and or vegan) along with sides and salads which come to £3-4 per meal. On the weekend, college does a great brunch for only £2-3 and dinner, which on Sunday's is usually a popular roast. In Cohen Quad, breakfast and lunch are available during the week for similar prices to the main site.

Formality: Exeter is more formal than some, but less than others. Whilst we are not allowed on the Front Quad grass, we can sit in the Fellows Garden which has an amazing view overlooking the Radcliffe Camera. We are one of the few colleges to have a black-tie ball every year, which everyone looks forward to at the start of Trinity Term and is the most affordable college ball in Oxford. Formal Hall dinners are held twice a week after normal dinners, where you can have a 3-course meal. For each subject, there is also an annual subject family formal dinner as well as special Formal Hall dinners for celebrations. Students must wear gowns at these dinners and it's also a nice occasion to dress-up more formally.

Grants and Bursaries: Exonian Bursaries are college financial assistance grants that are usually between £500-1,000. There are also some Hardship Bursaries available for those in need. Exeter also offer grants for books and equipment purchases, vacation study costs, travel for study or conferences, and internships. Funding for sports and arts activities is also available.

Location: Centrally located, a few minutes away from both the Radcliffe Camera and Bodleian libraries. Most departments are less than a 10-minute walk away. It's also great having so many restaurants, cafes and shops within a 5-minute walk, which saves a lot of time which makes a difference when you have a packed schedule and are trying to fit in as much as possible.

Politics & Reputation: Exeter is relatively politically neutral and known for being one of the most friendly and social colleges in Oxford. The size of each year is just over 100 people so you can recognise everyone and get to know lots of people quickly. As the college is quite small, when walking around Front Quad or going to the Bar you always run into a friendly face, which definitely makes catching up with people on a day-to-day basis easier and creates a more familiar and homely atmosphere.

Sport: Exeter has good sporting spirit and team bonding. Whatever, the sport, college cuppers teams get great support ranging from Men's football and rugby to more recently reaching the darts final twice in a row, and winning sailing cuppers! Every year we also have a sports day with our sister college in Cambridge, Emmanuel, which a huge number of people get involved with even if they've never played a particular sport before.

Green Templeton College

Founded: 2008

Famous Alumni: GTC has only been open for 12 years, so their alumni are still making their mark, and aren't quite famous yet.

Undergraduates: ~0 **Postgraduates:** ~600

Accommodation: There is some accommodation available on site but it had a distinctly undergrad feel. There is enough room for around half of the students at the college, and they are mostly accommodated off site, on Observatory Street or St Margaret's Road, or in new developments currently being finished further out of town. The best rooms to go for are in college if your priority is convenience, or in 5 St Margaret's Road if you want space and good facilities. Rooms are allocated by lottery, but it is best to contact the accommodations officer to check whether you can currently register for a lottery as lotteries are often announced on the lodge noticeboard and nowhere else, so they're easy to miss.

Bar: The Stables bar was recently renovated, and is a good place to have a drink or relax with some reading regardless of the time of day.

Price of a Pint: It's £1 for a bottle of beer (decidedly not pint-sized)

Chapel & Religion: The college is secular and has no chapel.

College Payment System: The college uses a credit system for dinners, but only takes cash at the bar, and things like laundry are only available via prepaid cards.

Food: GTC has a really well-established kitchen with a talented chef poached from a much older college several years ago. There is always a wide variety of food available from all over the world, and it's very rarely less than excellent.

Formality: GTC was only established in 2008, so it isn't big on formality or any of the things Oxford colleges are usually associated with. Formal dress isn't required at dinners with the exception of a handful of formals each year. In general, the college is liberal and open, there is little expectation of formality.

Grants and Bursaries: GTC is a young college with little by way of bequests at its disposal. There is a research fund available to all students of £200 per year, but financial assistance is otherwise offered on a case by case basis without any particular bursary or grant one can apply for.

Location: GTC is less central than many of the Oxford colleges, on the Woodstock road overlooking Jericho. This is in many ways advantageous, it is quiet at day and night, all through the year. The surrounding area is leafy, and it's a very short walk into Jericho or into the wilderness beyond.

Politics & Reputation: GTC, as a new graduate only college, is not widely known by Oxford students, its reputation is primarily one as a biomedical and policy research powerhouse, and often hosts global conferences on topics like public health. Politically, GTC is one of the most liberal colleges in Oxford, though as it matures this is gradually shifting.

Sport: GTC has an active (and successful) rowing team, among others, and inside the small campus we've also squeezed in some tennis courts and a state-of-the-art gym. There are a wide range of competitive teams and you can always contact the GCR representative for sport if you'd like to sign up!

Harris Manchester College

Founded: 1786

Famous Alumni: Roger Bannister, Peter Cruddas, Joseph Priestley

Undergraduates: ~100   **Postgraduates:** ~150

Accommodation: Accommodation in college is guaranteed for the first and final year of studies. All accommodation is in the college's beautiful historic buildings, and most rooms have en-suite bathrooms (otherwise bathrooms are shared between two). All students have access to communal kitchens within their house (some kitchens are shared between students in two houses). One of the houses is set aside for graduates only. Rooms are randomly allocated, except in your final year in which you will usually be allocated one of your top two preferences. Priority is always given to students who have accommodation related requirements owing to disabilities.

Bar: Harris Manchester is the only all mature students college at Oxford, but we still know how to have fun! - Harris Mancunians throw some of the best bops at Oxford. From legendary pub quizzes, real ale festivals, and open mic nights, Guest Nights, the JCR is a place to both hang out with friends and get the night started.

Food: All meals are served in the college's stunning Arlosh dining hall - on weekdays this includes breakfast, lunch, and dinner. Mondays and Wednesdays are Formal Halls when food is especially nice, wine is free, and gowns are worn! Sunday brunch is a student favourite, with living-in students chatting and feasting on a full English breakfast, many in pre-library pyjamas. The college's small size proves benefits here too: Oxford's loveliest kitchen staff knows not only your name but of course also your dietary requirements... from halal to vegan to gluten intolerant, you can be sure to be served your personal version of the meal's dish. Breakfast is £1.80, lunch is £3.75, and dinner is £5, but if you live-in, college meals (including Formal Hall!) are already included in your rent. For library snack cravings, you could always just head into the city centre, which is just a 5-minute walk away, and there is also the popular Alternative Tuck Shop which is just adjacent to the college.

Location: The college has moved around a fair bit through history, including as far afield as Manchester and York! It's now settled down in Oxford for the long term, roughly halfway between the parks and Christ Church meadow.

Hertford College

Founded: 1282 as Hart Hall

Famous Alumni: Fiona Bruce, Krishnan Guru-Murthy, Jeremy Heywood, Thomas Hobbes, John Donne, and many other politicians, presenters, writers, and scientists.

Undergraduates: ~400   **Postgraduates:** ~150

Accommodation: First year accommodation is pretty good, it's extremely central and most rooms are a good size, small gym onsite, though there are not many kitchens. Second year accommodation is a 15-minute walk out, not as pretty, no gym (though you can go to the one on the main site) but way more kitchens! Third year quite mixed, mostly houses, which can be really nice when you've matured and want to be a real adult.

Bar: Hertford is the only college with an underground bar. A student run bar, its décor is cosy with exposed brick. It is popular most nights of the week, and you can get a job working here in your second or third year.

Price of a Pint: ~£2.20

Chapel & Religion: Hertford has a beautiful college run by a very friendly Chaplain, Mia. It plays host to weekly services, to your matriculation ceremony, and also a wonderful choir – no audition required.

College Payment System: College bills are paid every term, including accommodation and kitchen fixed charge, like most colleges. Hall is paid for using your student card, and this is charged to your bills at the beginning of the next term.

Food: Hall serves three meals a day five days a week, with brunch on Saturday and Sundays. The food can be on the expensive side, at £4-5 for a meat main and side for dinner, though lunch is usually cheaper.

Formality: Hertford is a very friendly college with a strong community feel to it. A testament to this is that you're allowed to sit on the grass in Trinity (summer) term!

Grants and Bursaries: Hertford offers an extremely generous £1000 bursary for anyone with a household income of less than £53,000. This is more generous than most colleges I have seen! You can also apply for extra hardship grants, or sports funds for those on university teams.

Location: An extremely central college, convenient for most subjects. It is opposite Oxford's main, beautiful, library, the Bodleian, and adjacent to another beautiful library in the Radcliffe Camera. It is near exam schools, where many social science lectures are, as well as the Social science, Law, MFL and English libraries.

Politics & Reputation: Hertford is very liberal and open-minded as a college, and has had many Principals who have exemplified this. Its last Principal, Will Hutton, is a journalist and writer and nurtures the college's interests, particularly in his role working with the Hertford Economics and Politics Society.

Sport: Hertford's sporting success goes up and down with each cohort, as with most colleges. In recent years its women's boat club has seen huge success, as has its men's football team and joint Keble-Hertford women's football team. Sport at Hertford ranges from light fun to challenging and rewarding. If team sports aren't your thing, the gym and the yearly Oxford Half Marathon might be!

Jesus College

Founded: 1571

Famous Alumni: Harold Wilson, T.E. Lawrence ("Lawrence of Arabia"), John Richard Green, Magnus Magnusson, Sir Leoline Jenkins, Vivian Jenkins (Welsh Rugby Player), Norman Manley (Chief Minister of Jamaica), Kirsty McCabe, Hilary Lister (record-breaking quadriplegic sailor), and (very recently!) Kevin Rudd (Former PM of Australia)

Undergraduates: ~350   **Postgraduates:** ~230

Accommodation: Jesus offers accommodation for the every year of your degree – meaning that's one less thing you have to worry about! First years live in the main college site itself, where you will either have their own room or share a double set with one other person. Second and third years live in 3-4 person flats at the annex sites known as 'Stevens' and 'Barts' that are just a short cycle from college. Both annex sites have lovely garden spaces, and there's even a full size rugby pitch at Barts! Flats in the annex sites are allocated by a random ballot system, where if you are higher up in the ballot you have first choice in what flat you want. Accommodation can be a tad cold in the winter, but the college offers a heating subsidy to offset some of the cost of having the heaters on!

Bar: The Jesus bar (Baaa) was super recently renovated, and now features a karaoke machine, a UV room (complete with an Xbox and PlayStation!), and a foosball table. When there is a college event or a big club night on you can be pretty certain the bar will be full! The JCR committee also run a number of events in there (such as Thursday Karaoke pre-Bridge, pub quizzes, 'International Cocktail' Nights etc) which are always good fun.

Price of a Pint: ~£2.30

Chapel & Religion: Jesus has a lovely (albeit relatively small) chapel, which was the very first Church of England chapel in Oxford. That said, the chapel really is a place which welcomes people of all faiths and religions, and anyone is welcome to use the space, join choir, or attend Evensong regardless of their religion. Every Friday the JCR runs 'Friday @ 1' in the Chapel, which is essentially a super chill jam session for the musicians in college. The Chapel choir is non-auditioning, and all members get free weekly singing lessons!

College Payment System: Everything at Jesus (except the Bar) is charged to your termly batels – including rent, food, etc. If you receive a grant or subsidy from college this is subtracted off your batels so you just have to pay less. Normal Hall is charged on a per-item basis, but you are charged a fixed fee for the meal at 2nd Hall and Formal.

Food: Food is pretty good in Hall, and reasonably priced! There is always a veggie option, and the college is super open to hearing menu suggestions from students. There is also the 'Hatch' in the JCR where you can get coffee, chocolates and paninis if you fancy something a little lighter. '2nd Hall' runs 4 days a week and is 3 courses, and 'Formal' Hall runs only on Thursday and is 4 courses. 2nd and 3rd years also have full kitchens in their flats.

Formality: There are a few formal parts to student life, such as wearing gowns to Formal Hall. The JCR also runs a black tie event at the end of every term (which isn't compulsory, but almost everyone goes). But in general, Jesus falls on the more laid-back side of the spectrum!

Grants and Bursaries: Jesus is one of the richest colleges per student, which means they have a lot of money to help their students. There are loads of grants and scholarships offered, some of which are means-tested, and others are based on academic achievement. Particularly notable is the 'Dodd Fund', which awards every undergraduate a sum of money for non-academic travel at some point during their degree! The college Books Grant also pays students 75% off the cost of any books they buy for their degree.

Location: Jesus is smack bang in the middle of Oxford, located on the famous 'Turl Street'. There is a Pret just around the corner (where you will almost always find someone from Jesus grabbing a coffee) and Tesco is less than 5 minutes away. It is also only a 10-15minute walk to get to college from the train station or Gloucester Green Bus Station.

Politics & Reputation: Jesus is a super laid-back college, and is famed in Oxford for being one of the friendliest. Even our principal (Sir Nigel Shadbolt) often comes along to cheer on at our Sports games! It is known as the 'Welsh college' of Oxford, and definitely has more Welshies than the average college (though it's not like you'll be in a minority if you're not Welsh). Like most of the Turl St Colleges, Jesus is relatively politically neutral.

Sport: College sport is all about inclusivity – you don't need to be great at it, or even have played it before, to join. College cuppers are a big part of the College social calendar, and there is always a big turn out to cheer the Jesus teams on! Those who are more serious about their sport tend to aim for the Uni teams, and Jesus always has a number of Blues players across a variety of sports.

Keble College

Founded: 1870

Famous Alumni: Ed Balls (Former Shadow Chancellor), Imran Khan (Pakistan's Prime Minister)

Undergraduates: ~400+   **Postgraduates:** ~200+

Accommodation: For undergraduates - college accommodation is guaranteed in first and second year, and then students have a choice to 'live out' (in privately rented accommodation) in their third or fourth year. In general, enough students choose to 'live out' that college accommodation is available to third years who want it, but those on a four year degree will pretty much always have to move out for their final year (language students returning after a year abroad is the exception to this). All undergraduate accommodation is on the main college site, and most are en-suite (if not – you only share a bathroom with one other room). First and third years will live in the newer buildings, and second year accommodation is in the original college buildings. For graduates – there was a brand new accommodation block opened in 2019 across the road from the main college site which means accommodation can also now be guaranteed for first years, with some available for later years too.

Bar: Fondly referred to as 'the spaceship' – the bar was part of the 60s extension to the college – and is definitely retro but still a lot of fun!

Price of a Pint: £2.50ish for a beer, soft-drinks are £1!

Chapel & Religion: Keble was founded in memory of John Keble, who was a clergyman and theologian in the 1800s, so it was certainly founded as a Christian college, and has one of the biggest college chapels in Oxford. Today, some of the traditions remain (grace is said before formal meals, for example) – but it's not a big part of college life if you don't want it to be. The chaplain is a part of the welfare team for all students.

College Payment System: Food is charged to your student card, which is then paid off online at the end of every term alongside rent payments and any other college fees.

Food: Keble has regular 'formal' halls, at least twice per week plus Sunday (where students wear a gown over regular clothes and there's table service). There are informal halls (canteen-style) for the remaining dinners as well as breakfast and lunch. Food is quite reasonably priced, because only third-years have access to kitchens, and so eating in hall is a big part of Keble life. Breakfast includes a range of continental and cooked options, lunch will have cooked options (fish and chips, noodles, curry and rice) as well as jacket potatoes, pasta, salad, etc. Dietary requirements are catered for well, and there's an on-site café for lighter options like soup, sandwiches, paninis.

Formality: Keble had 'formal hall' for dinner every day up until very recently – and so it might seem like tradition is a big part of life here. But actually, it's one of the more relaxed colleges in the university, and traditions which are maintained are generally about bringing students together, rather than enforcing random rules!

Grants and Bursaries: The Keble Association offers a range of grants and bursaries for students with financial hardship, as well as study and travel grants. Funding is not quite as readily available to every student as it might be at wealthier colleges – but if you need it it's always there.

Location: Keble is about a 5-8 minute walk north of the city centre, and so manages to be close to everything you might need and still far enough away that it's not busy all the time. It's also right next to all the science buildings.

Sport: As its a big college Keble has societies for most major sports: football, rugby, cricket, rowing etc. as well as some more obscure ones like non-contact ice hockey played at 11.30pm twice a week! Rowing at Keble is well funded and well respected, and in general does quite well – with a number of rowers and coxes going on to star in The Oxford & Cambridge boat race over the last few years.

Kellogg College

Founded: March 1st 1990

Famous Alumni: Paul Bennett, Ruby Wax, Tom Mitchell, Grace Clough, Dom Waldouck, Jingan Young. Kellogg is particularly famous for its sporting alums.

Postgraduates: ~1140 Kellogg is graduate only. It is the largest college by number of students.

Accommodation: Kellogg has some of the best student accommodation in Oxford, and all their long-term accommodation have their own private gardens. The majority of the students are housed in three Victorian mansions, located on the Bradmore and Banbury Roads. The main campus has a lively MCR which organises a number of social events throughout the year, and a 24-hour library with adjoining study rooms. In 2017 the college hub was opened to provide an extra meeting space and café.

Bar: Kellogg sports a stylish modern bar, with events run by the MCR.

Chapel & Religion: Kellogg is a modern college with no chapel.

College Payment System: The college charges most things to students' batels accounts. The hub café is cashless, and all catering payments are made via the Upay system.

Food: The college dining hall serves lunches, dinners and special guest nights. Formal dinner is held once a week during term time. The hub café offers breakfasts, sandwiches afternoon tea and hot drinks.

Formality: Has an egalitarian ethos and boasts a lack of formality. It has no high table and no separation between students and fellows.

Grants and Bursaries: Kellogg offers several scholarships, including special scholarships for History, and the Hasmukh Patel scholarship for students from Africa.

Location: Much of Kellogg college was adapted from the 19th century Norham manor estate on the Bradmore Road. The centre of the college is now on the Banbury road, in a series of modern and Victorian buildings. The buildings are situated in the leafy and tranquil North Oxford, away from the centre of town, which is a short bus ride or 20-minute walk away.

Politics & Reputation: Originally founded for mature students; the college has since become one of Oxfords graduate only colleges. It is one of only three Oxford colleges without a royal charter and is officially a society of the University rather than an independent college. The college is very modern and has a huge international student population. The college was founded on St David's day, and uniquely at Oxford, grace is said in Welsh. The college has its own tartan which was designed by for Burns night by Robert Collins in 2013.

Sport: Kellogg has a strong reputation for sports and has produced a number of famous sportsmen, including several Olympians, several distinguished rowers and a few international rugby players. Kellogg has contributed rowers to the university boat race a number of times, and has its own punt on the river Cherwell. The college has their own football team in the MCR league.

Lady Margaret Hall

Founded: 1878

Famous Alumni: Benazir Bhutto, Michael Gove, Malala Yousafazi, and Nigella Lawson

Undergraduates: ~400   **Postgraduates:** ~200

Accommodation: As an LMH undergrad you can live in college for three years. Everyone has a kitchen near them and, even if not in first year, a large portion of the rooms have en-suite bathrooms. 1st years are allocated rooms together but all other year-groups are able to ballot for rooms with their friends.

Bar: The LMH bar is open every day until 11pm, with a happy hour from 7pm until 9pm. All of the staff are current students, and you can pay with your university identity (bod) card.

Chapel & Religion: LMH has an unusual Byzantine style chapel, in the shape of a Greek cross. There is a choir which is open to all, and carol services in the chapel in Michaelmas term.

Food: Hall is open for all meals Monday-Friday, Saturday brunch and Sunday dinner. The biggest culinary event of the week is formal hall on Friday: a delicious, three-course meal complete with candelabras and good company. The rest of the week eating in hall is a good way to relax and catch up with friends. A main meal cost around £2.50. There are always two vegetarian options and college are good at catering for dietary requirements.

Formality: LMH was founded as the first Oxford college to welcome women exclusively, and was the first to accept both men and women in 1979. The college is really proud of this tradition of inclusivity and tries to maintain a welcoming atmosphere for all. LMH is also unusual for having an official poet in residence.

Location: Nicely out of the centre of town, LMH is located just to the north of the university parks.

Sport: LMH has a wide variety of college sports teams. All LMH teams are open to everyone, from complete beginners to experienced blues athletes. LMH sports are mostly run on Facebook groups, so be sure to join in if you find yourself at the college!

Linacre College

Founded: 1962

Famous Alumni: Yasmin Alibhai-Brown, David Kelly, Neil Ferguson, Jef McAlister, Heather Couper, Keith Ward, Lady Gabriella Windsor

Postgraduates: ~550 (Linacre is graduate only)

ULTIMATE OXBRIDGE COLLEGE GUIDE | OXFORD COLLEGES

Accommodation: In addition to the onsite accommodation which houses the majority of students, the college owns flats, mainly on the Iffley road. The onsite accommodation features a number of rooms positioned around a central kitchen area. The college campus also has its own gym, private study rooms, conference facilities and impressive library. The college common room has its own Xbox, Nintendo Switch, darts board, Jukebox, camera equipment, bicycle maintenance kit and sewing machine. There is a pool table near the Tanner room.

Bar: Credited with the invention of two cocktails named the Major Corrections and Minor Corrections, respectively.

Chapel & Religion: Linacre does not have a chapel.

College Payment System: Most things are paid for via credit or debit card, or on the university batels system.

Food: Lunch and dinner is served in the dining hall, with guest dinners on Tuesdays and Thursdays. There are no meals served on the weekends. Linacre common room also sports its own BBQ. The college has its own veg box delivery service, which provides college members with local produce.

Formality: Linacre is a modern college and so is fairly informal, but college grace is still said in Latin. At the end of a meal all stand and say "Benedicto Benedicatur" -May the Blessed one be blessed.

Grants and Bursaries: Linacre has an academic hardship fund in addition to grants for academic excellence. There is also an academic activities fund for conferences and student led-seminars organised in the college. The Federick Mulder fund provides travel grants for those who work in a number of fields, including anthropology, social policy and refugee studies.

Location: Linacre's main campus is on the corner of South Parks Road. Much of the campus is 19th century, with recent new builds in the surrounding area. The main campus is next to the river Cherwell, and Merton college's playing fields.

Politics & Reputation: Linacre was Oxford's first Graduate only college, (and the UK's first for both sexes). It is famous for its Sexy Sub-Fusc bop, at which party goers wear their matriculation gowns in the most risqué way possible.

Sport: The college Punts are stored at nearby Wolfson College. Members have access to Oriel sports including their squash courts, on the Cowley Road. The college has a number of sports clubs, including the pleasingly named Linacre Ladies who Lift.

Lincoln College

Founded: 1427 by Richard Fleming, the Bishop of Lincoln

Famous Alumni: Dr Seuss, John le Carré, John Wesley Howard Florey, John Radcliffe, Emily Mortimer, Rachel Maddow

Undergraduates: ~301   **Postgraduates:** ~323

Accommodation: Accommodation is offered for all years of your degree. First year is on the main college site, second year is opposite the main college at the Mitre on Turl Street, and third and fourth years live ten minutes north, at Museum Road. There are also a number of smaller accommodation complexes for some fourth years and postgraduates.

Bar: Yes, Deep Hall or 'Deepers' is the legendary underground college bar, run by Simon.

Price of a Pint: £2.30

Chapel & Religion: Yes, we have a chapel which runs regular services and Sunday evensong with our wonderful choir. We also have an inter-faith prayer and quiet room.

College Payment System: We load our Bod cards with money at the start of each term which can be used in Hall and for non-alcoholic drinks/food in Deepers. This is rolled over from term to term but wipes at the end of each academic year. For those on the 'In College' plan the charge is £201.67 per term, for those on the 'Out of College' plan (including all graduate students) the charge is £88.

Food: Lincoln food has been known for decades as some of the best in Oxford. There are three meals a day served in hall six days a week, as well as a café lunch option and takeaway pizza from the bar in the evenings. The best meal is definitely Sunday brunch!

Formality: We have an informal hall every evening, and then a served formal hall after. This is smart casual and not particularly formal. Every other Thursday we also have a Great Hall, which is much smarter, and people tend to make much more of an effort. This is a great occasion and it always sells out!

Grants and Bursaries: There are plenty of college grants and awards for a variety of subjects and needs. We have: Senior Tutor's fund of up to £200 for academic activities, Vivian Green fund for projects of personal development, Travel Grants of up to £250 (extra for modern linguists) Books grants of up to £100 per year. There are also a large variety of scholarships and awards for academic achievement and contribution to college life (from £150 to £700), as well as substantial bursaries for those from lower-income households (ranging from £700 to £1333 per year). There are also a number of bursaries for special purposes such as extra expenditure incurred for your course.

In terms of sport, Lincoln has a 'Blues Fund' which assists towards the expenses of those who play in the University teams. Finally, there are JCR and College Financial Support Funds (Including a Gender Expression Fund) which aims to help students if they come into times of unexpected financial difficulty.

Location: Lincoln is one of 3 colleges on Turl Street, in the very heart of the City Centre. It is within 10 minutes of all major faculties and libraries, as well as less than 5 from the main shops.

Politics & Reputation: Lincoln has a reputation for being a very friendly and welcoming college, which is both progressive and yet still has some pretty interesting traditions. Both common rooms pride themselves in being apolitical. This, alongside with the wide variety of events put on by the college and common room officers means it has one of the tightest-knit and most diverse communities in terms of background. Perhaps for this reason, we are involved in a number of local charities and campaigns, fundraising for two charities per term. We boast a lot of college clubs and societies from sports clubs to history and music societies which help cement an extremely social community. Although Lincoln is small, it is known for punching above its weight in all aspects of wider university life and has recently experienced successes in all kinds of inter-collegiate competitions, from drama and music to sports. The main thing other colleges know Lincoln for is our library – which is supposedly the best of all college libraries! The library is the old city church on the corner of Turl, and so is a beautiful environment to study in, as well as being one of the dreaming spires. We also have a new college tortoise so are looking forward to dominating in the annual Corpus Christi Tortoise Race!

Sport: Lincoln as a college is extremely actively engaged in the wider sporting life of the University. Aside from free access to the University gym on Iffley Road, Lincoln shares a recently refurbished boathouse with Queen's and Oriel colleges in a prime location on the Isis in Christ Church meadow and have a variety of boats at all different levels. We also have an excellent sports ground at Bartlemas Road in Cowley with a modern pavilion, as well as access to tennis and squash courts for all students to use. There are a wide range of college sports teams for all levels, often with no experience required to join.

These teams are consistently extremely successful, especially given the comparatively small size of the college and we regularly reach the cuppers finals (university inter-college competitions) in a wide variety of sports. Each year, we also support a number of 'Blues', who are students of undergraduate or postgraduate levels who compete in their respective sports for the university itself, which often includes matches against other universities at some of the best sports pitches in the country.

Magdalen College

Founded: In 1458 by William Waynflete, Bishop of Winchester and Lord Chancellor.

Famous Alumni: Thomas Wolsey, Oscar Wilde, C.S. Lewis, Lord Howard Florey, King Edward VIII, Ian Hislop, Stephen Breyer, amongst many other writers, scientists, historians and Nobel Prize winners.

Undergraduates: ~400 (total), around 110 per year

Postgraduates: ~175 (total)

Accommodation: Accommodation is offered to all Magdalen (pronounced 'Maudlin') students for the entirety of their course, and vacation residence can be applied for. All first-year accommodation is outside the college grounds – it's a bit grim, but you learn to love your first uni room! Almost all second-year/all third-year rooms and onwards are in the beautiful college grounds right next to the deer park (yes, we have a deer park, with actual deer!) and all have sinks. Some lucky third years have en-suites. All undergraduate accommodation costs the same and is a decent price thanks to subsidising by the college.

Bar: The bar (called the Old Kitchen Bar, or the OKB) is reasonably large, with comfy seating and good wifi. This is where bops (college parties), general meetings, karaoke and other fun events are held.

Price of a Pint: £2.30

Chapel & Religion: The Magdalen College chapel is a Grade I listed building, dating from 1480, and is open as a place of worship for people of all beliefs. The regular choral and said services held in the chapel are Anglican and include a beautiful Evensong every Tuesday to Sunday.

College Payment System: You pay for your accommodation and a set rate for catering using your student loan/bank transfer into the college bank account at the start of each term.

ULTIMATE OXBRIDGE COLLEGE GUIDE | OXFORD COLLEGES

Food: The Old Kitchen Bar is open every day and serves good, sustenance food at lunch (paninis, customisable salads, pastries and daily specials like fish n chips) and pizza that can be ordered in the evening. The food in Hall is alright but can be quite expensive for 'subsidised' food. You pay for what you take (£3.00 - £4.00 per meal) and can get three meals a day there from Monday to Saturday. If you like to cook for yourself, there are good kitchen facilities available to all students, and nearby kebab vans for late night munchies! Fancy formal dinners are also offered at £9.00+ per person from Thursday to Sunday (Sunday formal is a special event – you get serenaded by the Magdalen Choir!), with up to five guests allowed per Magdalen host.

Formality: Magdalen is an old college with its own traditions, including the 500-year-old May Morning tradition of the choir singing from the top of the Magdalen Tower. These events give you a wonderful sense of Oxford's history, and Magdalen is otherwise very open and understanding; students are allowed to walk on the grass in Trinity (summer!) term, bops are allowed to continue until relatively late compared to other colleges, and we have a 'late gate' specifically for students who have stayed out too late to get back in through the Porter's lodge (main entrance).

Grants and Bursaries: Magdalen College offers financial support to around a quarter of its undergraduates in the form of the student support fund, which ensures that students can complete their course without having to worry about finances. Freshers are given £150 at the start of the year to buy academic materials, in addition to another £100 available for academic materials that can be applied for annually.

Location: Magdalen is just across from the Botanic Gardens, at the end of the High Street. Although not the most central college, Magdalenites are a short walk away from central Oxford and are also in a good position to explore Cowley, a diverse area of Oxford with lots of cafes, small restaurants and culture-specific supermarkets.

Politics & Reputation: Magdalen is an old, wealthy college, and has acquired a reputation for being a college for privately-educated, conservative students. This should not be seen as a barrier for anyone thinking of applying; the political views and backgrounds represented by the modern student body are far more diverse than this. Everyone is welcome at Magdalen, and the admissions statistics are being improved by the efforts of the college access and outreach teams year on year.

Sport: All Magdalen College students have free membership to the Iffley Sports Centre (including a regular gym, weight-lifting gym and swimming pool) a 10-minute walk from college. We have something for everyone in terms of sports clubs, from football to ice-skating to mixed lacrosse, with both casual and more advanced groups. Of course, we also have a men's and a women's boat club, with a designated rowing gym in the basement of the Waynflete Building (the main first-year block!).

Mansfield College

Founded: 1886

Famous Alumni: Adam Curtis. Pamela Sue Anderson. Chris Bryant. Guy Hands. Adam von Trott. Michael Pollan.

Undergraduates: ~239   **Postgraduates:** ~173

Accommodation: Accommodation at the college for all undergraduate students for all three years. Though some undergraduates still live out in college accommodation in Cowley (the Ablethorpe Building). There's also a couple of college owned houses that fourth-year students tend to live in. College accommodation is pretty good – most of the rooms are en-suite, though some of the biggest and nicest rooms aren't. There's some variation in quality but you get better choice as you progress through the years.

Bar: Not really. Mansfield claims to have a bar. It does physically have a bar. But the bar is almost never open. As in it opens a few times a term. Every so often groups of students will try to improve the bar and make it open more often – this invariably fails due to the opposition of the SCR. It is more accurate to treat Mansfield as not having a bar

Price of a Pint: When the bar opens, you can get a bottle of beer for about £3.

Chapel & Religion: There is a chapel, but it's also used as the canteen/dining hall – indeed, people call the dinner is called 'chapel'. But they do still have services there. It was originally founded for Nonconformists, and so has Nonconformist roots. The Prime Minister, Harold Wilson, was a Nonconformist and got married in Mansfield Chapel.

College Payment System: Online. You can pay with food with your university card ("bod card").

Food: High quality. Particularly good for vegetarian food, and was voted the best college in Oxford for vegetarian food. However, the food is relatively expensive (in part because Mansfield is one of the poorest colleges, so can't subsidise the food as much) – a dinner typically costs about £5.

Formality: Comparatively informal. It's a mostly state school college, and is relatively new, so there's not a great degree of formality. There are formal dinners twice a week and if you go to them you are expected to dress formally. Apart from that there's not really anything particularly formal.

Grants and Bursaries: Mansfield is one of the poorest colleges and, as a result, is not particularly strong for Grants and Bursaries. There are a couple of travel grants, and a hardship fund, but other colleges are much more generous in this regard. Having said that, there are quite a few prizes and scholarships for strong academic performance.

Location: It's located on Mansfield Road, which is pretty central. It's right next to University Parks which is great. It's about a five minute walk to the Bodleian Library, and about 10 minutes to the main central shopping area.

There's a great sandwich shop about 3 minutes away. It's one of the more central colleges.

Politics & Reputation: Mansfield is well-known for its high state school intake, so that it's basically the only college where the ratio of state school to private school students matches that in the general population (i.e. it's the only one that achieves fair representation, and doesn't skew in favour of private schools). It also typically does well on BAME admissions. As a result, it's a very inclusive college, and typically quite welcoming. It doesn't really have any of the elitism that Oxford is often accused of. Students tend to be fairly progressive, but it doesn't have the extreme progressive politics that places like Wadham have (it's a fairly moderate college). There are relatively few students with conservative views. Some students with conservative viewpoints have felt their political opinions are not fully respected, but these have also been very popular, well-liked students, so there's no real social exclusion based on politics (as there is at somewhere like Wadham). So it's known for being quite friendly and welcoming. However, as with the no bar thing, it's not typically a particularly 'fun' college. It's also the case that the SCR (i.e. the professors and administrative team) are far more paternalistic than at other colleges.

Sport: Doesn't have its own gym, but you do get free access to some of the university gym. Rugby and football (and possibly other sports) are played with Merton and on their pitches, in teams called the M&Ms. The sports pitches are pretty close, about a ten minute walk from the college.

Merton College

Founded: 1264

Famous Alumni: T.S. Eliot, J. R. R. Tolkien, Roger Bannister

Undergraduates: ~291   **Postgraduates:** ~244

Accommodation: Provided for all years. First year in College, second year in Holywell St (central Oxford), final year in College.

Bar: A little dilapidated last time I checked, but friendly, cosy and cheap. Plenty of quizzes, karaokes and general buzz towards the end of the week.

Price of a Pint: £2.50 for a Carlsberg

Chapel & Religion: The chapel is often host to Evensong, with a strong choir, excellent acoustics and new organ installed in 2013.

College Payment System: Food is on a PAYG basis using your library card to scan in.

Food: Cheap, generally good and lots of it. Meals are non-itemised, so you can have a main, or a main, dessert and unlimited salad and it doesn't make a difference to the cost.

Formality: Quite traditional - gowns must be worn to all meetings with the Warden, and there is the option of formal hall 6 nights a week – but it's BYOB! Quirky ceremonies such as the Time Ceremony (look it up) make tradition fun there.

Grants and Bursaries: In plentiful supply – Merton is one of the richest colleges and people don't take enough advantage of the travel grants, books grants etc. Monetary prizes are always awarded for good performance in termly exams.

Location: Best of both worlds – you're 2 minutes from the High Street and 5 minutes from Cornmarket St, but tucked away on the cobbled Merton St you can barely hear a car go by.

Politics & Reputation: No real political atmosphere. Due to regular residency at the top of the Norrington Table it's known as the college 'where fun goes to die.'

Sport: Not a particularly sporty college, but home to a small in-college gym, squash courts, tennis courts and expansive playing fields at the sports pavilion. And one of the UK's only 'real tennis' courts...

New College

Founded: 1379

Famous Alumni: Hugh Grant, Kate Beckinsale, H.L.A Hart, Sophie Kinsella, Susan Rice

Undergraduates: ~421   **Postgraduates:** ~368

Accommodation: Accommodation is provided to all 1st, 2nd and 4th year undergraduates, with most first year accommodation being en-suite. The way accommodation is allocated is through a housing ballot. The first-year room which assigned to you is ranked on a ballot, and those with a 'worse' room in first year, get given higher priority to choose their 2nd year room. This works really well because it means that everyone pays the same price for their accommodation. In 3rd year, the majority of students live in privately rented accommodation, although there is some accommodation available in college should you need it. 4th year students live in 'Sacher' building or '21 Longwall' where they have access to a kitchen. Unfortunately, the majority of 1st and 2nd year accommodation has no kitchen access and is catered – although the food in hall is delicious and going to dinner is a great way to get to know people!

Bar: Our bar has recently been renovated and has an old, castle-like feel to it. In the day, it operates as a café where you can work, get reasonably priced coffee and have a chat with our friendly baristas! This does mean it has a less 'bar' like feel than some other colleges, but it's still a nice place to go in the evenings. We host pub quizzes in the bar, darts competitions, and it's a popular location for sports teams to gather for drinks!

Price of a Pint: £2.50 (a real steal compared to your average Oxford pub)

Chapel & Religion: The chapel is beautiful, with our renowned choir singing nightly services (except Wednesday) called 'evensong'. This can be really relaxing to go to, no matter what beliefs you hold. The chapel itself is Church of England, however it hosts a catholic mass once a term. There's also daily morning prayers (which end in time for morning classes), this is followed by a free breakfast in hall. The Chapel is also used as a venue for concerts, other services, and lectures. Recently, we had a talk given by Baroness Hale in the chapel, as a celebration of the 40th anniversary of women being admitted to New College.

College Payment System: Payments for accommodation and catering is done through 'batels'. This is a lump sum which is paid to the college and it is possible to add things such as club tickets in freshers week, bottles from the wine cellar and guest night spaces onto your batels. Anything extra which is put onto batels, is then added to next terms batels for accommodation and catering. Your bod card (essentially your student card which gives you access to libraries etc.) can be topped up with money as well. This is used to pay for breakfast/lunch/the bar, and it can be topped up as and when needed.

Food: The dining hall at New College is stunning and definitely has the Hogwarts feel to it. It was also the setting for 'When I kissed the teacher' from Mamma Mia 2! The food itself is great, with our head caterer Brian Cole always being keen to take on board student feedback. There is an 'early hall' sitting each evening of the week, which is a self-service style meal. The prices of the standard evening meals are £7.23. Then three times a week, there is the option to go to 'formal hall' – a three-course, waiter service meal in hall, where gowns are worn. The food at formal hall is really nice and sitting down to have a three-course meal with your friends is a great end to the day. The price for this is also £7.23. Then, every week (although this alternates between the JCR and MCR so is effectively fortnightly) there is guest night. Guest night is also a 3-course, waiter service meal with tea and coffee but it is fancier than formal. No gowns are required but guests dress up and it's a great occasion to bring your family and friends to, with the food being of excellent quality. This costs £19.25.

Formality: New college is not that formal, with a very friendly and homely feel to it. Our formal halls are not formal at all, with the only requirement being that a gown is worn (even if over tracksuit bottoms!). There is, of course, the opportunity to get dressed up for guest night if you wanted to.

Grants and Bursaries:

These are available to students from certain Oxfordshire state schools who are offered an undergraduate place at the University.

The Nick Roth Travel Award (worth £500) is in memory of former undergraduate, Nick Roth, who died in an accident whilst travelling in South America. The Morris Long Vacation Travel Grant (worth £1000) is generously funded by an Old Member of the College. These grants are given out generously by the college for students and you apply for them by outlining the academic merits of your travel.

There is also the China Travel Award which gives students up to £1000 for travelling to mainland China.

The College also supports students taking fast-track language courses at the Language Centre, by reimbursing half of their course fees. The 'Sports and Cultural Fund' can also be applied to for expenses incurred through participating in sports, or culture, for example, music and drama where the college reimburses up to half of the expense.

Scholarships and Exhibitions are awarded to recognise outstanding academic achievement. They are usually made at the end of first year, following first year exams. If you win a Scholarship you will receive £400 each year; for an Exhibition you will receive £275.

Location: New College is primely located on Holywell Street, giving it fantastic access to the law faculty, the English faculty, the science buildings and town. Tesco's is around a 10 minute walk maximum from college, with the major libraries and other faculties being between 5-15 minutes away.

Politics & Reputation: The undergraduate body is called the JCR (Junior Common Room) and the MCR (Middle Common Room) is the graduate body. Both the JCR and MCR have committees which are headed by a president. On those committees, there are financial officers, welfare officers, ethnic minorities officers, LGBTQ+ officers, disabilities officers, access officers, charity officers, environment and ethics officers and women's officers etc. The committee is elected by the JCR and MCR and fortnightly meetings occur where motions are brought and voted on regarding college issues and how to spend the JCR and MCR budgets.

Outside of college politics, New College is not known for any particular political affiliation. The student body tends to be quite keen to discuss social issues, for example access to Oxford, climate change and there are weekly discussion groups on women's issues.

New College has a strong academic reputation, consistently coming near the top of the Norrington Table (used to rank college academic attainment) and is also known for being quite a wealthy college. It is also generally a very friendly community, which is especially apt given the college motto is 'manners maykth man'!

Sport: New College has a great variety of college sport to get involved in. There is rugby, rowing, football, lacrosse, squash, hockey, netball and other sports such as Dancesport, tennis and cricket. Our sportsgrounds are conveniently only a five minute walk always from the main college site, a big bonus of the college when contrasted with some. College sport is really welcoming towards all levels, so is a great way to make friends and try a new skill!

Nuffield College

Founded: 1937

Famous Alumni: Mark Carney, Michael Oakeshott, John Hicks, Manmohan Singh

Undergraduates: ~0   **Postgraduates:** ~80

Accommodation: The college provides on site accommodation for first and second year students, including a few flats for couples. As probably Oxford's smallest college, Nuffield has more generous accommodation for postgraduate students than most.

Grants and Bursaries: On a per student basis, Nuffield is Oxford's richest college, which means they offer generous funding packages, including full fee bursaries for all students, research grants, and office space.

Location: Right in the centre of town, just behind Oxford Castle on the new road.

Politics & Reputation: Nuffield is the hub for social science research at Oxford, and has been the centre of many developments in econometrics. It's a pretty brainy place, and with a lot of fellows and students engaged in political questions, there's always lively discussion.

Oriel College

Founded: 1326

Famous Alumni: Sir Walter Rayleigh, Alexander R. Todd, Rachael Riley

Undergraduates: ~320   **Postgraduates:** ~200

Accommodation: You can, if you choose to, live in college residence for the full duration of course. First and second-year undergraduate accommodation is in the college, whereas third and fourth-year undergraduate and postgraduate accommodation is on Rectory Road, roughly a 15 minute walk from the college.

Bar: The bar is small, but always full of friendly faces. There's a pool table, darts board, and a TV with Sky Sports.

Price of a Pint: £3

Chapel & Religion: Oriel chapel is Church of England, though it is warmly welcoming to everyone. Choral evensong is the main service of the week and takes place on Sundays. Morning prayer takes place every weekday, and compline every Wednesday.

College Payment System: Oriel uses the 'batels' system: students scan their university card when paying for food in hall, or printing, and are then emailed a bill to pay, which includes accommodation expenses, at the start of the next term. Balance on your 'batels' can be checked at any time online, so it's easy to track your spending.

Food: The food is reasonably priced. £4 for a huge cooked lunch (including pudding!), £6 for 3 courses at formal dinner. The food isn't extraordinary, but it is nice, and they cater well to dietary requirements.

Formality: Formal dinner requires all students to wear their gown over a dress or dinner suit. Other than that, Oriel is fairly casual.

Grants and Bursaries: Sports grants are awarded to half blues (£50) and blues (£100) each year. Bursaries are available to students from low-income families. On top of that, if a student is struggling with money, or they have encountered sudden expenses, they can apply to the college for a bursary.

Location: High Street. Very central! Short walk to shops, libraries and many departments.

Politics & Reputation: Oriel has a great reputation for its rowing success. Politics of the college is very conservative, and has drawn controversy over its Cecil Rhodes statue, which the 'Rhodes Must Fall' movement believes should be removed.

Sport: Rowing is incredibly well funded by Oriel. With free coaching, access to excellent equipment and an enthusiastic atmosphere, it's no wonder Oriel rowing has been, and still is so successful. Oriel also has football, Netball, Rugby and croquet teams, but these are much more relaxed.

Reuben College

Founded: 2019

Oxford's Newest College: Reuben College was only founded last year, so it doesn't have any students yet, let alone alumni! An all graduate college, it will take in its first students in autumn 2021. If you're reading this, and find yourself there, please visit the Uni Admissions website, get in touch with our editors, and tell us all about this new college!

Pembroke College

Founded: 1624

Famous Alumni: Samuel Johnson (compiled the first English dictionary), Michael Heseltine, Pete Buttigieg, Victor Orban (Prime Minister of Hungary), Abdullah II of Jordan. Sir Roger Bannister (first man to run a mile in under 4 minutes) was Master of the College in the 1980s. J.R.R. Tolkien was the Professor of Anglo-Saxon at Pembroke in the 1920s.

Undergraduates: ~350   **Postgraduates:** ~250

Accommodation: Undergraduates are guaranteed 3 years of accommodation, although more is possible. At least one year will be in the annexe, which is only a 5 minute walk from the main site. There are 6 "bands" of room which vary in price: cheaper ones tend to be smaller, while more expensive ones will have an en-suite and larger beds. Students rank their preferred bands and locations, and the college uses a ballot system to see who gets first pick. A lot of the nicer rooms on main site have term-time only contracts.

Bar: Not as popular or actively used as in some of the other colleges, although the JCR has been making an effort to increase footfall by hosting open mic nights. **Price of a Pint:** £3

Chapel & Religion: The chapel is beautiful, and has a very different feel to a lot of other chapels due to the ornate and rich decoration inside. It is open during daylight hours for anyone who needs a place for quiet reflection, regardless of their beliefs. There are weekly Sunday services, and a very open and friendly Chapel choir, who also get free formal dinner afterwards!

College Payment System: Your college card can be used to pay in Hall, the Bar, and in Farthings, the college cafe. The Bar and Farthings also take contactless cards. Lunch in Hall is paid by item, whereas dinner has a flat price. All first years are required to attend dinner in Hall; if there is a Formal option that night, they must attend that one unless you get prior approval (e.g. university sports club training) to attend Informal Hall that night. You have to pre-pay the price of these dinners (~£350) at the start of term. From second year onwards if you live on main site, you have the choice of remaining on this meal plan, or pre-paying a little more (~£370), and then spending that money either in Hall or in Farthings throughout the term.

Food: Hall food can vary a lot in quality, but is fine most of the time. The college brownie which is sometimes served for pudding is fantastic, and loved by many students. Wednesday dinners in Hall are meat-free. Farthings food is very good, especially the bagels.

Formality: Pembroke is not as formal as many other colleges. Formal Hall is available (and compulsory for first years) 3 times per week in the first term, 2 times per week in the second, and once per week in the third. Undergraduates are required to wear their gowns to hall, but not black tie.

Grants and Bursaries: Pembroke has a reasonable financial support scheme, and the staff are very friendly and helpful. However, it's not a very rich college, and this sometimes shows. The Rokos Awards are particularly useful for science students who wish to undertake practical research work in the holidays.

Location: Pembroke is across the road from Christ Church and is pretty central, but is also not obvious in its location - many people walk by without realising that the college is there!

Politics & Reputation: Pembroke is relatively small and not as well-known as many other Oxford colleges. The JCR itself is the richest JCR in Oxford, so it often donates to charities in response to political events.

Sport: College sport is very strong in Pembroke, especially the Rowing Club. One of the few college clubs in Oxford that is completely free, Pembroke often boasts one of the largest numbers of crews entered into college competitions. Pembroke was also the first ever college to secure a double headship - coming first in both the men's and women's races in the Summer VIIIs Headship.

Regent's Park College

Founded: 1927, when the college moved to Oxford

Famous Alumni: Not very many to be honest.

Undergraduates: ~120.   **Postgraduates:** ~50.

Accommodation: Regents offers accommodation for first and third year students only. People live out in second year, usually in Jericho which is quieter and closer to the centre than Cowley but also more expensive. The college accommodation is all on the Pusey Street main site and all the same price for every room (very reasonable- much cheaper than living out). The room sizes vary a lot and you can either end up with a lovely, big room overlooking the quad or a vile box room looking out onto some bins. Third years live in shared flats on site. There are kitchens to share with everything you need. The college is generally very good at allowing people to stay over the vacations (for an extra fee)

Bar: Voted the best bar in Oxford, Regents bar improved my life in so many ways. It is small and grotty but really fun and one of the last student run bars in Oxford. They also have a tab system and card machine which is great, so you can always get a drink even if you have no money. The selection of booze is surprisingly good and they make some awful 4-5 shot cocktails for about £3? Ridiculous but makes clubbing so much cheaper, and a good place to bring people back to.

Price of a Pint: £1.00-1.50

Chapel & Religion: As a Baptist college, Regents has a significant religious presence and a very active (if not super pretty or old) chapel.

College Payment System: The admin staff are good and it's easy to pay batels by bank transfer or by card machine.

Food: The food is largely terrible in my opinion. That being said, it's on the cheap side and has a number of vegetarian options

Formality: Very informal. Everyone is friendly and approachable, and the welfare team and academic administrator are amazing and always vouch for their students. People who get into difficulty with their faculties are almost always backed up by the college.

Grants and Bursaries: Although a small and poor college, Regents is fairly generous with travel grants offering several up to the value of £250, which are quite easy to get compared to other colleges as there are less people competing for them. The JCR also offers sports and arts grants, for example to study a language or put on a play, which are again quite generous and offered every term. People who run into financial difficulty are supported for example by discounted vacation residence.

Location: Opposite St John's, Regents is very centrally located right near to Tesco and all the libraries, but also slightly tucked away. Especially well located for Oriental Studies, Theology and Philosophy students.

Politics & Reputation: Regents is very public school heavy. I was one of only a few state school students in my year, and traditionally Regents has a reputation for being rowdy and posh (Bullingdon club was founded at Regents, apparently...). Although politically I would say it's a mix which is nice. In the years below it seems that the private vs state school number of students is becoming more balanced I think, and the college has a genuinely very friendly and welcoming environment.

Sport: Has taken off in recent years. The college has a netball team, a football team and a rugby team joint with Mansfield and Merton. The rowing teams are active but I don't think they do very well at a university level due to the small pool of people.

Somerville College

Founded: 1879

Famous Alumni: Margaret Thatcher (Britain's first female PM), Indira Gandhi (India's first female PM), Dorothy Hodgkin (first British woman to win a Nobel prize in Science).

Undergraduates: ~400   **Postgraduates:** ~200

Accommodation: Somerville is located about 10 minutes walk from the city centre. Accommodation is located in several buildings inside the College. All undergraduate students are guaranteed on-site accommodation for the duration of their 3 or 4 year degrees. Rooms are a good size. Most first year students live in Vaughan, which is a concrete brutalist building. Most first year accommodation has bathrooms and kitchens shared between rooms on each floor. However, some rooms for finalists have en-suite bathrooms (Radcliffe Observator Quarter buildings). There is a gym on the ground floor of Vaughan that students can use after an induction session for a reasonable price.

Bar: The college bar is called 'the Terrace' and is located on the first floor of Vaughan. There is an indoor and outdoor section- the latter is lovely during the summer. There is also a very popular pool table, which costs 50p/game. There is a good selection of beers (including a few local ones), wines, spirits and unique college cocktails.

Price of a Pint: ~£2.50

Chapel & Religion: Somerville has a nondenominational chapel that hosts events and services from a variety of religious affiliations. Past speakers have included Christian bishops, Rabbis, Daoists and Atheists. Every Wednesday during Michaelmas term a Mindfulness Meditation session is held at 6pm in the Chapel- these sessions are free and open to all members of college.

College Payment System: All payments are handled online via EPOS. College bills are called Batels, and these are paid every term- this includes accommodation charges. You can also top up your college card with money on EPOS, that can be spent in the college dining hall or in the bar.

Food: Hall serves three meals a day Monday-Friday, with brunch and dinner Saturday and Sunday. Full meals with dessert usually cost around £4-5. Some days are now 'meat-free' as part of the student body's efforts to reduce the college's environmental impact.

Formality: Somerville is an extremely relaxed and liberal college, where you can be free to express your opinions and thoughts. Most tutorials are similarly relaxed and informal. In contrast with many other colleges, Somerville has a large central grass quad that you can walk and sit on all year! In the summer, some tutorials even take place outside in the sun.

Grants and Bursaries: The University offers Oxford Bursaries and Crankstart Scholarships based on annual income for UK/EU students. Somerville College offers several undergraduate Thatcher Scholarships for UK/EU and overseas students based on academic excellence. Overseas students are considered for these after being offered a place to study, while UK/EU students are considered following their first public examination (usually at the end of first year). This scholarship covers 100% of University fees and provides a very generous grant towards living and travel expenses. Similar scholarships are also available for graduate students.

Location: Somerville College is located in Jericho, which is about 10 minutes walk from the City Centre. The location is ideal- it avoids much of the hustle and bustle of the city centre, but is also very accessible. Its neighbours are St Anne's College (across the road from the main entrance) and Green Templeton College. The maths department lies right next to college, and the Medical Sciences Teaching Centre (where almost all preclinical medicine teaching takes place) is an 8-minute walk/4-minute cycle away.

Politics & Reputation: Somerville is a very liberal college, and is keen to platform all views. However, the student body is mainly left wing, even though our most famous alumna is Margaret Thatcher!

Sport: There are many options for getting involved in College sport. The essential Oxford sport is rowing- it involves very early mornings and freezing fingers, but the camaraderie is fantastic. The two big college regattas are Torpids (Hilary term) and Eights (trinity term). Somerville has an extremely strong women's boat club- it holds the record for most Headships (overall victories) in both Torpids and Eights. Somerville also has teams for more mainstream sports (football, hockey, rugby, netball, cricket) and more niche ones (croquet, pool, table tennis and squash).

St Anne's College

Founded: 1879

Famous Alumni: Mr Hudson (rapper and R&B artist), Tina Brown (editor of The Daily Beast and ex-editor of Vanity Fair and The New Yorker), Danny Alexander (former Chief Secretary to the Treasury), Sir Simon Rattle (principal conductor of the Berlin Philharmonic). Dame Iris Murdoch became a fellow in 1948 and taught philosophy at the college until 1963.

Undergraduates: ~400   **Postgraduates:** ~300

Accommodation: Undergraduates are guaranteed 3 years of on-site accommodation. All undergraduate bedrooms are single occupancy, almost half of which are en-suite, and all accommodation includes kitchens shared by approximately 9 students. Students on four-year courses, except for linguists who spend a year abroad, usually live out for one year in college-rented houses or subsidised private rentals.

Bar: The college bar is a popular spot at the weekend, after formal dinners and before bops. It houses a pool table, table-football, quiz machine, dart board, juke box and is used for charity pub quizzes. **Price of a Pint:** £2.50

Chapel & Religion: St Anne's is a secular college and opted to build The ST Anne's Coffee Shop (STACS) instead of a chapel.

College Payment System: University cards or 'bod' cards can be used to pay in the bar, STACS and hall. Once you pay your college fees at the start of term, your bod card will have a balance of £125 – if you use this up before the end of the term, you can top it up online. The bar and STACS also accept cash and bank card payments.

Food: St Anne's chefs have won awards in national competitions and cater to all dietary requirements in hall. Hall serves breakfast, lunch and dinner on weekdays and brunch at weekends. There is always a vegetarian option and quite often a vegan option and weekly menus can be found online at the beginning of every term. A range of wraps, sandwiches and snacks are available at STACS if you miss hall mealtimes.

Formality: St Anne's is an informal college. Formal hall takes place around 5 times a term and does not require attendees to wear gowns.

Grants and Bursaries: St Anne's has a number of bursaries and travel grants available to students, and finance staff are helpful when anyone experiences any unprecedented hardships.

Location: St Anne's is north of the city centre – 5 minutes by bike – by the University Parks and close to the Science Area, Ashmolean Museum, Modern Languages and Classics Faculties and Mathematical and Oriental Institutes, as well as the Radcliffe Observatory Quarter. It's not a traditional-looking college, but this adds to the down-to-earth atmosphere.

Politics & Reputation: St Anne's is not a well-known college, but it is a friendly and inclusive community and offers a supportive and informal co-educational environment to students of all backgrounds.

Sport: St Anne's has college teams for badminton, cricket, rounders, football, hockey, netball, rowing, rugby and tennis. These are open to all experience levels and serve as a great opportunity to meet people – the hockey team, the rugby team and the women's football team are also joint with other colleges!

St Antony's College

Founded: 1950

Famous Alumni: Richard Evans, Thomas Friedman, Gary Hart

Postgraduates: ~500

Accommodation: St Antony's has 104 rooms, which are mostly reserved for first-year graduate students, although there are some rooms available for continuing students as well. Many rooms are en-suite, and all have access to full kitchen facilities.

Formality: St Antony's College is an unusual college, as it focuses almost exclusively on International Relations, with the college itself structured around seven regional research centres. Like other graduate only colleges, St Antony's is relatively informal, meaning that you'll be mixing as peers with leading academics on a day to day basis. Students share many facilities with fellows on equal terms, and there is open seating in hall.

Location: Located in central Oxford, the college has great access to all university facilities.

St Catherine's College

Founded: 1962. Although its roots go back to 1868 when the college was a delegacy for unattached students.

Famous Alumni: Benazir Bhutto, Peter Mandelson, J. Paul Getty, John Vane, Paul Wilmott, Jeanette Winterson

Undergraduates: ~500

Postgraduates: ~420

Accommodation: St Catz' main campus was built in 1962 by Danish architect Arne Jacobsen, created with a traditional quadrangle layout, but using new materials. Jacobsen incorporated the gardens into his quad design, making St Catherine's a particularly green and pleasant college. The campus has a range of onsite accommodation, including newer modern en-suite rooms, older en-suite rooms, and box rooms with a sink. A further 42 rooms are located at St Catherine's house on Bat Street. The college campus itself is one of the largest and has a wide range of facilities. The JCR is one of the biggest in Oxford, and has dart boards, arcade games, table-football, pool tables, a Nintendo Wii and a Sky Sports television. The campus has a large library and computer room, and a well-equipped and spacious gym.

Bar: The JCR bar is cheap and well-stocked, and has a very impressive whiskey and liquor selection. **Price of a Pint:** £1.50

Chapel & Religion: St Catherine's is a secular college and does not have a chapel.

College Payment System: Meals are paid for via the Upay system, using the university card.

Food: St Catherine's is a fully catered college, providing meals all day. Dinner has two sittings, "Scaf" a cafeteria style informal dinner, and the hall dinner, which has a more extensive menu.

Formality: Formal halls are held on Wednesdays and Sundays, for which there is a fairly strict dress code and code of conduct, which includes a strict limit on alcohol consumption and a ban on singing and shouting.

Grants and Bursaries: The college has a hardship fund and provides bursaries for students from low income households. Other grants include a grant for medical textbooks, and grants for academic excellence for graduate students.

Location: Tucked away down Manor Road, although St Catz is not in the centre it is only 5-10 minutes from the high street. The college is five minutes from the University parks and the Bodleian library.

Politics & Reputation: St Catherine's has recently performed very well in the inter-collegiate Norrington Table. It is the youngest Undergraduate college, and as with all the modern colleges has a less traditional and more egalitarian reputation. Due to the lack of tourists, it is one of the more tranquil grounds in Oxford. The college's motto is 'Nova et vetera', the new and the old.

Sport: St Catherine's has a well-equipped (and free) onsite gym, and is a short walk away from one of the larger rugby pitches. St Catherine's is known as a sports college and is popular with students looking to get involved in wide variety of sports. A number of Olympians have rowed for the college.

St Cross College

Founded: 1965

Famous Alumni: Jonathan Orszag, Tim Foster, Hermione Lee

Postgraduates: ~500

Accommodation: St Cross has 187 rooms, mostly for first-years, after that you're expected to live out. There are a few rooms available if you want to apply for them in later years, but they are allocated by a ballot. Many rooms are en-suite, and all have access to full kitchen facilities.

Formality: St Cross is one of the least formal Oxford colleges, and has the smallest professorship to student ratio, meaning that you'll be mixing as peers with leading academics on a day to day basis. Students share most facilities with fellows on equal terms, and there is open seating in hall.

Location: Located in central Oxford, the college has great access to all university facilities.

St Edmund Hall

Founded: Uncertain; teaching began on the site as early as the 1190's but is estimated to have been established in 1236. However, the name 'St Edmund Hall' (or affectionately, Teddy Hall) did not appear in writing until 1317. The Hall received official Oxford college status (as it was previously known only as a 'Hall') in 1957. So, oddly, it is both the oldest and the youngest Oxford college! Women were first admitted as members of the college in 1978.

Famous Alumni: Al Murray, Keir Starmer, Bishop Micheal Nazir-Ali, Stewart Lee

Undergraduates: ~400   **Postgraduates:** ~250

Accommodation: All first-year students live on the main site. Most third- and fourth-year students (by ballot) live in college owned property, the college is quite physically small (although not in student number) so many of the third- and fourth-year students live off of the main site, but all property is within easy walking distance of the college. The accommodation is varied and there are four main accommodation areas. Two (Whitehall and Besse) are more stereotypical student accommodation buildings, with long corridors and small communal areas. One building (Kelly) has smaller floors but many of them, and is supposedly the tallest building in Oxford without a lift! This building has larger communal spaces and is lived in by first-year students (although some first-years do live in the Whitehall and Besse). The front Quad also provides accommodation for third- and fourth-year students (and for special cases, second-year students). This has very varied room sizes and facilities, so is very much a luck of the draw when selecting a room there! In second-year, the vast majority of students live out in Oxford in houses that they select in the first/second term of first-year. Graduate students typically live in their own privately rented properties, or in the Norham Gardens building, one of the furthest from college site but on a very nice and quiet road in Oxford.

Chapel & Religion: The college is christian, with an active choir. A small but very active religious community exists in the college, with students and staff alike dedicated to running events and providing pastoral care.

ULTIMATE OXBRIDGE COLLEGE GUIDE | OXFORD COLLEGES

College Payment System: Online portal to termly 'Batels' with the option to add additional funds for washing/food etc. This is easy to use but tends to be on the expensive side.

Food: Very good, particularly for formal dinners. Plenty of choice (including for vegetarians!) Meals are more expensive than in many colleges, but are worth it if you enjoy good food!

Formality: Formal dinners bi-weekly, requiring gowns and formal dress. At normal meal times and in/around the college however it is generally very informal. Usually no dress code is needed for academic meetings (e.g. tutorials). There are events such as meeting the principle early on in first term which require dressing up smartly, so be sure to bring formal clothes!

Grants and Bursaries: Available from internal and external funds for those with financial difficulties, as regular payments or one-off's. There are also bursaries to cover sports equipment costs (if competing at varsity level) and grants of £100-£300 for education resources (easily accessible).

Location: Next door to Queen's college, at the bottom (North) of the High Street, next to Longwall Street. Location is perfect for access to academic facilities (5-10 minutes' walk from almost all libraries), as well as getting to town (same distance to Westgate shopping centre). This location is also good for when living out in 2nd year, the majority of properties are in Cowley which is only 5-15 minutes' walk from the main college site.

Politics & Reputation: College politics are present but you don't have to be involved if you don't want to. The JCR (junior common room) and adjoining student bodies have the funds to put on events and trips so being involved in those can be rewarding. Reputation of being a fierce sports competitor and a boisterous college atmosphere. The latter is true to an extent, but it can be largely avoided if undesired.

Sport: Famous for rugby, with a huge internal following in college. Teddy has a strong rowing team and the students are very into pool (although this is only run as an intra-college, unofficial competition).

St Hilda's College

Founded: 1893

Famous Alumni: Susanna Clarke, Zanny Minton Beddoes, Val McDermid

Undergraduates: ~400   **Postgraduates:** ~170

Accommodation: Accommodation at St Hilda's is provided for first and third years. This means second years live out in shared houses, often on Cowley road and the area close to it. This isn't as scary as it sounds though, and many students look forward to the chance to live independently for a year. First year accommodation is allocated at random and all rooms are the same price to make it fair. There are shared kitchen and bathrooms for each floor, but both are sufficiently big to avoid any problems of space or competition. If you have a good reason not to share, the college is happy to make alternative arrangements.

Bar: We have one of the few surviving student run bars in Oxford. This means it is fairly cheap, with nights like 'pound a pint' Thursdays, and 'Drink the bar Dry' at the end of each term. The Entz team runs bops, with themes like 'Disney' and 'Charity Shop BOP.' We've had wine and cheese tasting nights, and have recently bought a large chest filled with board games for student use, alongside our pool table and table football.!

Price of a Pint: £1

Food: The set-up for food at St Hilda's is fairly informal compared to most colleges. It is the only college with round tables which makes for much more sociable meals. Canteen-style breakfast, lunch, and dinner is served Monday to Friday, whilst brunch is available on Saturday and roast dinner on Sunday. This means that you don't have to sign yourself or any guests in for meals, (you just turn up), and you can pay for exactly what you eat rather than a set price for a three-course meal that you might not want. If you wanted to experience Formal Hall, there is still the option to attend one on Wednesday nights. If that's not your thing, however, you can always grab a takeaway from the hall that day too!

Formality: St Hilda's was the last college at Oxford to admit men, letting them in since 2008. The college is one of the few where you can walk on the grass! It's much more relaxed than the average Oxford college, which is a relief if you've been in the city centre all day and need somewhere to escape to!

Location: A short walk from the High Street, St Hilda's is on the edge of East Oxford, just over Magdalene Bridge.

St Hugh's College

Founded: 1886

Famous Alumni: Emily Davison, the suffragette died for the cause at the 1913 Epsom Derby, Theresa May, the former UK Prime Minister, Aung San Suu Kyi, Former State Counsellor of Myanmar.

Undergraduates: ~420   **Postgraduates:** ~377

Accommodation: St Hugh's accommodates its students for all 4 years, all for a fixed price. Older years get to pick their rooms first, but in a random order. All accommodation is on the college site. In second year you can usually choose to live in a staircase of 8 or in a set of 2 (sharing a bathroom and kitchen). In 3rd and 4th year you are likely get an en-suite, or you can choose to live in one of the houses onsite (a really good experience of living in a house without having to live out of college).

Bar: The bar is just below the JCR, and is where college bops are held. The drinks are a bit cheaper than the spoons in town. The bar is usually not very busy unless there is an event on, but the people will usually bring drinks up to the JCR where the atmosphere is better. **Price of a Pint:** £2.40

Chapel & Religion: The chapel is quite small, but the chaplain and his wife are very involved in student welfare and keen to help out. You can join the college choir, which practises once a week and performs at Sunday evensong. There is one service a week.

College Payment System: You pay with your University Card for food, which you can top up online.

Food: We have 2 places for food, hall which is open for breakfast, lunch and dinner 5 days a week and offers brunch on the weekend. A full meal will cost you about £3, there is a different meat, veggie and vegan option every meal, all of good quality. There is also the Wordsworth Tea Room which offers a higher quality lunch and breakfast 5 days a week, for around £5 this is a nice treat.

Formality: Hugh's formals are once a week for £10. These are well regarded around the university, and offer a delicious 3 course dinner. The dress code for this is dress suits for boys and girls will usually wear a dress or something similarly smart.

Grants and Bursaries: Hugh's does make sure to offer a lot of grants and bursaries to its students that need it. You can get money from the hardship fund should you come into difficulty financially throughout your degree, and college are always keen to help with any financial or welfare issues.

Location: The location is treated as Hugh's downside, but you really grow to not notice it. It's about a 20 minute walk to the centre of town, although a lot of departments are closer than this. It's about a 5 minute cycle if you get a bike, which I'd recommend. It does mean that we do not have tourists wandering the grounds, and we have the space to have loads of beautiful gardens that you're allowed to walk in. It's a highlight working on the grass in the summer with no interruption.

Politics & Reputation: St Hugh's is a bit of a left-wing college, trying to get the university to raise its standards and looking after student welfare.

Sport: Although it may not be top of the league in any sports (nearly in pool), but St Hugh's is the only college that will have a 20 person turn-out, day drinking and chanting, for a completely random college football game. Rowing is a big sport within the college, completely open to beginners, with a really fun atmosphere and 2 women's and men's boats. There are 2 men's football teams, one women's football team, 2 netball teams, and teams for badminton, cricket, rugby, lacrosse and more. Having a kick-about on the lawns in summer is also lovely.

St John's College

Founded: 1555

Famous Alumni: Tony Blair, Rupert Graves, Philip Larkin, Victoria Coren

Undergraduates: ~450   **Postgraduates:** ~200

Accommodation: for all years of undergraduate and plenty for postgrads too! First years are split into two but half the year lives all together in one accommodation block with the other half in another quadrangle. Second years can ballot for a shared house owned by college on a road just behind college - so still very convenient location-wise - and third/final years get top pick of rooms from old with lots of characterful wooden beams to brand new with en-suites and spacious kitchens.

Bar: Yes - with a French sommelier as the barman! Lots of fancy cocktails, Japanese whisky, Polish vodkas and regular open mic nights. There are two pint-sized college cocktails too which are great value for money (the Saint and the Sinner). People from other colleges are frequently very impressed at the number of different drinks on offer and the willingness of the barman to customise cocktails to personal taste - all for so much less money than the average bar in Oxford.

Price of a Pint: £2.40

Chapel & Religion: Yes - Anglican chapel but multi-denominational services throughout the year including termly Catholic mass. There is a chapel choir that does evensong twice a week but the chapel is also sometimes used as an events space, such as for art exhibitions.

College Payment System: you top up your university card online to pay-as-you-go for meals and in the bar. You pay your termly accommodation via bank transfer and it is always possible to pay for food/drink with cash too.

Food: Three meals a day in hall, 7 days a week plus brunch on Sundays, formal dinner 4 days a week and a café open 11-3 for food every day. Guest dinners are also a real highlight - twice-termly four-course meals with a fancy dress black tie dress code. Unlimited Prosecco beforehand and unlimited port afterwards with a professional photographer, it is a highlight for John's students and their friends and family who can be invited along.

Formality: John's is a fairly formal college but has a fair-sized state school intake which meant it felt very welcoming for me. We have formal dinners several times a week and a very valuable wine cellar, along with some very imposing architecture but the overall vibe is very friendly!

Grants and Bursaries: £350 a year academic grant for laptops, books, etc. Travel grants available as well as university level sports grants and more! For example, as a languages student, I was lucky enough to be given £800 to spend a month in Lisbon improving my Portuguese. The college gives lots of money to students putting on productions and is able to loan/gift money to students who find themselves in financial difficulty.

Location: Very central! Two minutes from Tesco and the Ashmolean and the nearest nightclub, slightly more to University Parks, John's is convenient for basically everything. And there is a bike scheme which allows students to take out bikes if they need to travel more quickly between classes/sports matches etc.

Politics & Reputation: People often describe John's personality as non-descript and even though it's the richest Oxford college it certainly doesn't feel particularly right-leaning. It is also lesser known among tourists so it certainly retains a student over a tourist atmosphere. I was dissuaded from applying to some of the more stereotypically 'posh' colleges and I definitely don't feel out of place at John's.

Sport: squash courts, two gyms (one weights-based, one cardio-based), rowing erg room, bike scheme. The is a sports ground about 1.5 miles up Woodstock Road where the rugby and football teams play their fixtures but training often takes place five minutes away at University Parks which is very handy.

St Peter's College

Founded: 1929

Famous Alumni: Ken Loach, David Davies, High Fearnley-Whitingstall

Undergraduates: ~340   **Postgraduates:** ~100

Accommodation: College house you onsite for the first two years of your degree, then you can choose to live in one of the College owned properties in North Oxford or live privately in your final years.

Bar: Voted the best bar of any university college in 2015, the bar is student run and much more affordable than most others.

Price of a Pint: £1.80

Food: The pay as you go food in hall can range from around £2.50 to £6 with a permanent salad bar alongside the other 4 or so main options offered, which range from steaks to Mediterranean vegetables and tofu stacks. There are always vegan, gluten free and vegetarian options, with possible allergens highlighted clearly. A full English breakfast is available everyday, and brunch at the weekends,

Formality: Formal hall is on Tuesday and Thursday nights with BYOB and a nice three course meal for £7.50. As a whole the college is fairly informal, as one of the smaller and newer colleges.

Sport: The college has sports teams competing in rowing, cricket, football, table football and rugby. It shares with Exeter and Hertford Colleges a sports field which has two cricket pitches and pavilions, two rugby and football pitches, a hockey pitch, tennis courts and a squash court.

The college boat club, St Peter's College Boat Club, competes regularly. The club shares a boathouse with Somerville College, University College, and Wolfson College Boat Club, which gives students a chance to mix with the grad students at Wolfson.

The Queen's College

Founded: 1341 by Robert de Eglesfield, and is named for its first patron Queen Phillipa of Hainault, the wife of Edward III.

Famous Alumni: Henry V, Oliver Sacks, Tony Abbott, Tim Berners-Lee, Walter Pater, Ruth Kelly, Jeremy Bentham

Undergraduates: ~Queen's is one of the tiniest colleges with less than 400 undergraduates. **Postgraduates:** ~Queen's only admits 75 graduate students a year.

Accommodation: All undergraduates are offered college accommodation for the duration of their course. Much of the college was designed by Sir Christopher Wren and Nicholas Hawksmoor and features some stunning neoclassical architecture. The better rooms have en-suites, and the others have shared communal bathrooms. There are no kitchens in the college accommodations, but everyone tends to eat in the dining hall anyway. Room sharing is available to reduce fees. All first year undergraduates are housed in the main campus. Second years onwards are mainly housed in buildings surrounding the college. Every accommodation building has its own common room. The college has a very good JCR, with a Sky box and DVD collection. The college has its own gym and squash courts. The onsite library is very large and the upper library is world famous.

Bar: The Beer cellar bar is one of the most popular and highly rated college bars in Oxford. Housed in the basement, it has a catacomb-esque feel.

Price of a Pint: £2

Chapel & Religion: Queens has a spectacular chapel built in 1364. It has a number of important architectural features including beautiful stained-glass windows dating from 1518. The chapel was largely rebuilt in the Baroque style during the 18th century. The chapel is home to Queen's College Choir, one of the more famous and prestigious choirs at Oxford University.

College Payment System: Queen's uses the university batels system for payments. Food and drink can be bought using the cashless Upay system.

Food: Queen's is a fully catered college with breakfast lunch and dinner served every day in the dining hall. The JCR serves teas, coffee and cakes. The dining hall has two sittings a day, the second of which is done in academic gowns. Saturday formals include a three-course meal in formal attire.

Formality: Queen's is an old-fashioned formal college with a high table. College grace is said in Latin before dinner, and at important dinners grace is sung by the choir.

Grants and Bursaries: The Crankstart scholarship is available for students whose household income is less than £16,000 per annum. The college also provides the Hawley fund, for the funding of activities which will directly help the student's future career.

Location: Queens is in the centre of Oxford off the high street, and so maintains a party atmosphere on the weekends. Queen's is one of the more popular colleges with tourists, and can get very busy in the summer.

Politics & Reputation: Queens has a reputation as one of the friendlier and more fun colleges, defying its antiquity. The college traditionally has links with the North of England via its founder Robert de Eglesfield, although nowadays it sports students from everywhere. It is one of the smaller colleges and known for a more intimate feel. Queen's is particularly well-known for its music, with an excellent choir, orchestra, and jazz band.

Sport: The college has one of the world's oldest boat clubs and is credited with participating in the race which would one day become the Henley Royal Regatta. Queen's has its own sports grounds including two heated squash courts, arguably the best in Oxford. Queen's is one of the few colleges with its own gym.

Trinity College

Founded: 1555

Famous Alumni: William Pitt the Elder, Dame Sally Davies, Bonnie St. John, Jacob Rees-Mogg

Undergraduates: ~300   **Postgraduates:** ~100

Accommodation: College houses you onsite for the first two years of your degree, then you can choose to live in one of the College-owned properties in North Oxford or live privately in your final years.

Bar: The Trinity Beer Cellar is an underground bar famous for its whiskey collection and the College drink, the Unholy Trinity (to be consumed at one's own peril!) **Price of a Pint:** £2 - £4 depending on how fancy you are!

Chapel & Religion: Choral evensong is in chapel every Sunday, and the choir rehearses regularly. There are some occasional weekday services to mark special occasions.

College Payment System: College offers you 3 meals a day in Hall, which you can pay for on your University card which works on a pay as you go system.

Food: Really good! Trinity is famous for having the best food in Oxford, and steak and brie night on a Monday is always fully booked.

Formality: Friday night dinner is a very formal dinner, where you can bring a guest and get a lovely four course dinner for £18, a bit more than the normal £4 for a formal where you can wear jeans and trainers as long as you remember your gown and stand up for grace!

Grants and Bursaries: Subject specific grants are available throughout the year for travel or research, college offers all students an annual books grant.

Location: Couldn't be more central! Broad street is slap bang in the city centre, a quick walk away from lecture halls, libraries and cafes.

Politics & Reputation: People don't usually think of Trinity as being a small college, but it definitely is in terms of numbers, which means that although some people think of it as being stuffy or old fashioned, it definitely isn't!

Sport: College sport is a big part of the Trinity community and is open to all interests, we have a great joint rugby team with Wadham, a girls' netball team, hockey and for the less physically inclined, the annual Beer Cellar Triathlon (table football, darts and pool).

University College

Founded: 1249

Famous Alumni: C.S. Lewis, Percy Shelley, Stephen Hawking

Undergraduates: ~300   **Postgraduates:** ~100

Accommodation: Undergrads get accommodation for every year of their course. Accommodation for undergraduates in 1st and final year is normally on the main site whilst 2nd and 4th years will be offered accommodation at the annexe in North Oxford, or at another College-managed property within Oxford. After first year, students ballot for rooms, and so can choose who to live with. There's a variety of room sizes but all of them have WiFi, a sink, desk and mini-fridge, and the rent stays the same. Most rooms have shared bathroom and kitchen facilities, but the brand new rooms in the Goodhart building have en-suite bathrooms. As a postgraduate student, you are guaranteed accommodation for your first year of study.

Bar: There's usually three bops a term, and the first of the year is always the famous toga bop... Bring a spare sheet! Bops are held in Univ's spacious bar, which was also redone recently so is stylish and has a really relaxed atmosphere. Univ also hosts a phenomenal summer ball every other year.

Food: Univ usually offers 3 meals a day in hall during term time, except at the weekend when there is brunch instead of breakfast and lunch. Meals cost £3-4, and the portions tend to be huge so you get pretty good value for money! There's always a vegetarian option and at least two meat/fish choices. In case you fancy cooking for yourself, facilities for self-catering are available! Formal Hall is three times a week, and Sunday Formal is always busy because it's free for the choir.

Location: In the middle of everything on the High Street.

Wadham College

Founded: 1610

Famous Alumni: Christopher Wren, Rowan Williams, Michael Foot, Rosamund Pike, and Felicity Jones

Undergraduates: ~450   **Postgraduates**: ~200

Accommodation: College house you onsite for the first and third years of your degree, and in the new Dorothy Wadham Building on the Iffley Road in second (and fourth) years.

Bar: The Wadham Bar hosts regular queer bops for LGBTQ* students, and all student events end with the playing of Free Nelson Mandela. The bar entrance has a mosaic designed by Wadham mathematician Roger Penrose!

Food: Lunch is served in the new refectory each weekday, and usually costs £2-4. Half the options are vegetarian! For dinner (which is £4.27) you can eat either in the new refectory or in hall if you're feeling fancy. Wadham doesn't do formals, but there are guest nights where students can bring parents or friends.

Politics & Reputation: Wadham is one of the most liberal colleges, and was the first to fly the rainbow flag for Pride in 2011. The college also has a longstanding relationship with Sarah Lawrence College in the US, where 30 students from SLC come to Wadham to study for a year, with 6 Wadham students going in the opposite direction each spring.

Wolfson College

Founded: In 1966 by the great Liberal philosopher Isaiah Berlin, a college exclusively for postgraduates.

Famous Alumni: Artur Ekert, Chris Whitty, Richard Ellis, Alison Gopnik

Undergraduates: ~N/A   **Postgraduates:** ~500

Accommodation: Wolfson owns some of the most modern accommodation in Oxford, both on site and around the campus. The off-site housing is located in the poshest and most expensive part of Oxford at reduced rates. Many of the on-site rooms have views overlooking the quad, duckpond, punt harbour, or college gardens. The college has an on-site nursery, as its members are on average much older than the other colleges.

There is a small library which is open 24 hours a day, a bar, games room, and sports facilities. Wolfson's common room is particularly comfy, and boasts an excellent selection of magazines and newspapers, and free coffee is available at regular intervals. Wolfson's upper corridors are home to some incredible works of modern art, including drawings by M.C. Escher, all of which may be rented by students who wish to have them on their bedroom walls.

Bar: Wolfson's excellent cellar bar was set up as a co-op style social experiment, in keeping with the college's political reputation. Bartenders work on a voluntary basis, and as a result it is one of the cheapest bars in Oxford. It has an adjoining games room for table tennis, table football and dart. A number of bops are held here throughout the year.

Price of a Pint: £2.90

College Payment System: Most things are paid through the college batels system. Batels, card and cash are all accepted forms of payment in the dining hall.

Food: Wolfson provides meals every day in its dining hall. There is also a small café which provides snacks and sandwiches. The college has an excellent wine cellar, and special wines are available upon request. Tea and coffee are available in the MCR, and is frequently free at regular social events and coffee mornings.

Formality: Wolfson is famously informal and is popular with those who dislike the pomp and circumstance of other colleges. Isaiah Berlin founded it with an egalitarian ethos in mind. There is no High table, so fellows and students mix at dinner and during social events. There is also only one common room.

Grants and Bursaries: Wolfson has a number of scholarships available for academic excellence, particularly in the fields of physics, philology and history. They also award sports grants for talented sportsmen, to offset travel costs incurred when travelling to and from sports competitions.

Location: Located on the River Cherwell in the North of Oxford, Wolfson is the furthest away from the centre of Oxford of all the colleges. The college provides a free minibus service for those tired of walking into the centre. It is the site of Oxford's Punt harbour. There is a private boathouse and restaurant next to the college, the Cherwell Boathouse, which is extremely popular on summer evenings for its beautiful views of the river. The closest pub is the Rose and Crown, famous for its pint glass full of sausages and lovely beer garden.

Politics & Reputation: Founded by the famous Liberal philosopher Isaiah Berlin, Wolfson is known for being one of the more politically radical colleges and is sometimes nicknamed the "Berlin Wall". Wolfson bar is home to the Communist Party Party, a very popular bop. There is no high table, one common room for all members, and gowns are rarely worn.

Sport: Boasting an onsite gym, squash court, croquet lawn, and nearby playing field, Wolfson is strong for sports and is particularly known for its boat club. Wolfson has a day of sporting contests every year against its sister (and enemy) Darwin college, Cambridge. This usually includes a serious drinking competition and the theft of oars from the enemy college.

Worcester College

Founded: 1714

Famous Alumni: Rupert Murdoch, Russell T Davies

Undergraduates: ~400   **Postgraduates:** ~200

Accommodation: Accommodation varies between different grades. Most will have a sink if no en-suite, with different buildings for different years. You can ballot with friends for 2nd year onwards, and a points-based system is used to ensure fairness over the years. Accommodation is only guaranteed for 3 years of your degree, although it is possible to have accommodation for 4 years.

Bar: Worcester has a small bar where college bops, quiz nights, karaoke nights frequently take place. There is a snooker/ pool table and a quiz machine in there too.

Chapel & Religion: We have a college Chapel which holds regular services, on most days, as well as extra services for special occasions. The college choir sing in these services.

College Payment System: Upay cashless system, we use the app or website to add money to the account, which then goes onto our Bod card and we can tap this for payments for food.

Food: Hall meals served 3 times a day, plus brunch on a Sunday, and formal hall sittings 4 times a week

Formality: Very informal. All staff are incredibly friendly, tutors will frequently offer you tea when you have tutorials with them, and everyone is on first name terms.

Grants and Bursaries: Worcester college has a Travel Fund which students of any discipline can apply to. There is also a Hardship Fund but this is normally a last resort. Reading grants of up to £100 are also available to any undergraduate over their degree course.

Location: Very central, right next to the Ashmolean Museum, and the language faculty library, and Tesco's. Also just up the road from the train station (15 mins walk).

Politics & Reputation: Known as a very tight-knit, friendly college. No particular political orientation.

Sport: Worcester has many sports teams that don't require experience, including a rowing team.

ULTIMATE OXBRIDGE COLLEGE GUIDE — PERMANENT PRIVATE HALLS

WHAT IS A PPH?

If you've been researching Oxford colleges you'll have come across PPHs, or Permanent Private Halls. You shouldn't confuse these with halls at other universities, which normally just means a block of flats where the first years all live together. Permanent Private Halls are a uniquely Oxford thing, and even then, most Oxford students won't know much about them.

There are six PPHs at Oxford, and each of them was originally founded by a different Christian denomination. There are different from colleges, in that rather than being governed by the fellows of the college, they are in part run by the relevant Christian denomination.

All students are PPHs are full students of the university, and are no different from colleges as an academic experience. Regent's Park College, the largest PPH, is listed along with the other colleges in this collection, as it accepts students of any age or gender for a range of undergraduate courses.

Campion Hall only accepts Jesuit priests, and other mature students who are already ordained priests. Blackfriars, St Stephen's Hall, and Wycliffe Hall only accept graduate students, and only a hundred or so between them, so we've not included them in this collection, as we couldn't find anyone studying at them to contribute! As you'd expect, these PPHs mostly cater to students studying Theology and related subjects, so unless you're planning a career in the clergy, they won't be relevant to you.

Several Oxford colleges, St Peter's Hall, Mansfield and Harris Manchester became full colleges in the last few decades after being PPHs, so if you find yourself being interviewed there, it's a good point to bring up to show that you've done your reading!

Few students apply directly to PPHs, fewer than 100 in 2020, so most students will have been pooled to them. Be reassured that a PPH is still the full Oxford experience, and that if you're feeling cunning, they do have a very slightly higher acceptance rate than other colleges in the most recent data at least!

ULTIMATE OXBRIDGE COLLEGE GUIDE — PERMANENT PRIVATE HALLS

WHICH COLLEGE QUIZ

This quiz is a little bit of fun but also a small aid in helping the undecided decide. Note down the answers to your questions and sum up the frequency of each letter to see which colleges we recommend. Be honest with the answers you select!

1. **Where would you most like to be based during your time at Oxford or Cambridge?**
   a. Not quite in the busiest part of the city, but close enough to be anywhere in 10 to 15 minutes by bike or walking
   b. Right in the city centre
   c. In a quieter area of the city with fast routes into the centre
   d. Further out of the city with its own community
   e. I don't mind where I'm based

2. **What kind of atmosphere would you most like in your college?**
   a. Small and close-knit where everyone knows each other
   b. A large space and a lot of people
   c. Lots of activities taking place, but with a relaxed atmosphere
   d. Lots of people, but everyone has their own niche
   e. Relaxed and a bit different to the usual Oxbridge college

3. **How do you feel about the Oxbridge traditions (e.g. formal hall, gowns)?**
   a. I like them, but I don't want to have to embrace all the traditions
   b. I love the idea, it's all part of the experience
   c. I like a few traditions but I don't want to be too stuck in the past
   d. I would rather avoid Oxbridge traditions
   e. I would welcome some traditions, especially the more unusual ones

4. **What is the least important factor you would consider when choosing your college?**
    a. The extra-curricular activities and facilities
    b. The competition for places
    c. The location
    d. The traditional Oxford experience e. Academic excellence
    e. The accommodation arrangements
5. **What would you want to do in your free time?**
    a. Spending time with friends from college
    b. Attending formal hall
    c. Playing college sport
    d. Getting involved in drama and music societies or politics groups
    e. Lots of different things – I enjoy a range of activities

Mostly As

You like the idea of going to an old, renowned college where you can have the traditional Oxbridge experience, but you would prefer somewhere small with a close-knit community. You would like the peace and quiet of being somewhere tucked away but still want to have easy access to the centre of the city and university.

Considering Cambridge?

Explore these colleges: Corpus Christi, Peterhouse, Sidney Sussex.

Considering Oxford?

Explore these colleges: Brasenose, Blackfriars, Corpus Christi, Lincoln, Mansfield, Queen's, Regent's Park, St Edmund Hall, St Benet's, St Stephen's House, Wycliffe Hall.

ULTIMATE OXBRIDGE COLLEGE GUIDE | **PERMANENT PRIVATE HALLS**

Mostly Bs

You want the traditional Oxbridge experience – the gowns, formal dinners, playing croquet on the college lawn – and for the opportunity to discuss your favourite topics with likeminded people. You want to be in the centre of everything and have the opportunity to make your mark during your time at university.

Considering Cambridge?

Explore these colleges: Christ's, Downing, Gonville and Caius, Jesus, Magdalene, Queens', St John's.

Considering Oxford?

Explore these colleges: Balliol, Christ Church, Exeter, Magdalen, Merton, New, Oriel, St John's, Trinity, Worcester.

Mostly Cs

You love the old buildings in Oxford and Cambridge, but you don't want to study somewhere that is too archaic. As much as you like some traditions, you would like somewhere with a more liberal outlook where the traditions are just a small, fun element of day-to-day life.

Considering Cambridge?

Explore these colleges: Clare, Emmanuel, Girton, King's, Newnham, Pembroke, Selwyn, Sidney Sussex, St Catharine's, Trinity Hall, Wolfson.

Considering Oxford?

Explore these colleges: Hertford, Jesus, Keble, Lady Margaret Hall, Keble, Pembroke, St Hilda's, St Hugh's, St Peter's, University, Wadham.

Mostly Ds

The traditional Oxbridge experience is not that important to you – you would much rather have a modern college with state-of-the-art facilities, even if it is a bit further out of town. You would like everything to be laid-back, relaxed and forward-thinking. You are looking forward to getting involved in university-wide activities and meeting interesting people, and you want the college you attend to reflect that.

Considering Cambridge?

Explore these colleges: Churchill, Fitzwilliam, Homerton, Lucy Cavendish, Murray Edwards, Robinson, St Edmund's

Considering Oxford?

Explore these colleges: Harris Manchester, St Anne's, St Catherine's, Somerville.

Mostly Es

You don't mind if your college is old or new, big or small – you just want somewhere that has a bit of individuality. You are not worried about going to an academically rigorous college, you just want to embrace all that university has to offer and to go somewhere where you can be yourself. To you, going to Oxbridge is an opportunity to throw yourself into something new, meet interesting people and experience new things, both academically and socially.

Considering Cambridge?

Explore these colleges: Fitzwilliam, Girton, Gonville and Caius, Pembroke, Queens', Robinson, Sidney Sussex.

Considering Oxford?

Explore these colleges: Mansfield, Pembroke, Regent's Park, St Hilda's, Wadham.

FINAL ADVICE

Acknowledgements

Thank you to all the tutors who helped in in this mammoth project, including those not mentioned earlier in the text. We could never have hoped to produce this complete a resource without you!

An Appeal to Readers

We hope you've enjoyed this book and found it useful. We've done everything we can to avoid mistakes and inaccuracies, but even in institutions as old as Oxford and Cambridge, some things do change. If we've missed anything, made any errors, or just not been as positive about your college as it deserves, please get in touch with us at books@uniadmissions.co.uk.

We are always looking for current students to help us with our teaching, as well as to update books like this one. If you would like to become part of our network of tutors and contributors, please drop us an email, or sign up direct only the Uni Admissions website.

About Us

We currently publish over 85 titles across a range of subject areas – covering specialised admissions tests, examination techniques, personal statement guides, plus everything else you need to improve your chances of getting on to competitive courses such as medicine and law, as well as into universities such as Oxford and Cambridge.

Outside of publishing we also operate a highly successful tuition division, called UniAdmissions. This company was founded in 2013 by Dr Rohan Agarwal and Dr David Salt, both Cambridge Medical graduates with several years of tutoring experience. Since then, every year, hundreds of applicants and schools work with us on our programmes. Through the programmes we offer, we deliver expert tuition, exclusive course places, online courses, best-selling textbooks and much more.

With a team of over 1,000 Oxbridge tutors and a proven track record, UniAdmissions have quickly become the UK's number one admissions company.

Visit and engage with us at:

Website (UniAdmissions): www.uniadmissions.co.uk

Facebook: www.facebook.com/uniadmissionsuk

YOUR FREE BOOK

Thanks for purchasing this Ultimate Book. Readers like you have the power to make or break a book –hopefully you found this one useful and informative. *UniAdmissions* would love to hear about your experiences with this book. As thanks for your time we'll send you another ebook from our Ultimate Guide series absolutely FREE!

How to Redeem Your Free Ebook

1) Find the book you have on your Amazon

purchase history or your email receipt to help find the book on Amazon.

2) On the product page at the Customer Reviews area, click 'Write a customer review'. Write your review and post it! Copy the review page or take a screen shot of the review you have left.

3) Head over to www.uniadmissions.co.uk/free-book and select your chosen free ebook!

Your ebook will then be emailed to you – it's as simple as that!

Alternatively, you can buy all the titles at: www.uniadmissions.co.uk

Printed in Great Britain
by Amazon